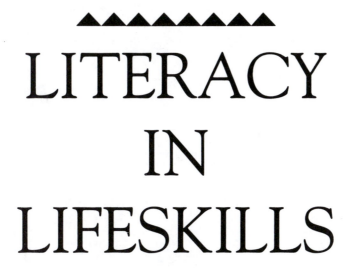

LITERACY IN LIFESKILLS

BOOK 2

LITERACY IN LIFESKILLS

BOOK 2

Sally Gati
City College of San Francisco

Heinle & Heinle Publishers
A Division of Wadsworth, Inc.
Boston, Massachusetts 02116 U.S.A.

Much love and thanks to my ever-helpful husband, Frank
and to my ever-supportive son, David.

Thanks, too, to Mary Kapp and to all
the teachers who, for over ten years,
tested these materials.

To all the students who were the reason and
inspiration for developing **Literacy in Lifeskills**
— a special thank you.

Publisher: Stanley J. Galek
Editorial Director: Christopher Foley
Assistant Editor: Margaret M. Morris
Production Supervisor: Patricia Jalbert
Manufacturing Coordinator: Jerry Christopher
Cover Designer: Brian Sheridan
Illustrations: Progressive Typographers, Inc.
Production Supervision: Progressive Typographers, Inc.

Heinle & Heinle Publishers is a division of Wadsworth, Inc.

Manufactured in the United States of America.

ISBN 0-8384-3907-1 (Book 2)

10 9 8 7 6 5

Contents

n a s x j
d i
z f
r
k
Lower-Case
e Letters
l
CHAPTER 1

▲▲▲▲▲▲▲▲▲

Lower-Case
Letters

o u

p b
g
y
v h
c t
q w m

1. Copy the letters.

C c C c

A a A a

D d D d

G g G g

O o O o

Q q Q q

S s S s

Copy the small letters.

c a d g o q s c a d g o q s

Copy the words.

1. dog _ _ _

2. dogs _ _ _ _

3. sad _ _ _

4. good _ _ _ _

2. Copy.

L l L l

B b B b

F f F f

H h H h

I i I i

J j J j

K k K k

l b f h i j k l b f h i j k

5. flag _ _ _ _

6. book _ _ _ _

7. bag _ _ _

8. fish _ _ _ _

9. kiss _ _ _ _

10. black _ _ _ _ _

11. ball _ _ _ _

12. socks _ _ _ _ _

13. big _ _ _

14. clock _ _ _ _ _

3. Copy.

M m Mm _____

N n Nn _____

P p Pp _____

R r Rr _____

T t Tt _____

U u Uu _____

m n p r t u mnprtu _____

_____

15. man _ _ _   20. chair _ _ _ _ _

16. fork _ _ _ _   21. no _ _

17. run _ _ _   22. spoon _ _ _ _ _

18. a big fish _ _ _ _ _ _ _

19. a small fish _ _ _ _ _ _ _ _

4. Copy.

V v   V v _____

W w   W w _____

X x   X x _____

Y y   Y y _____

v w x y   v w x y _____

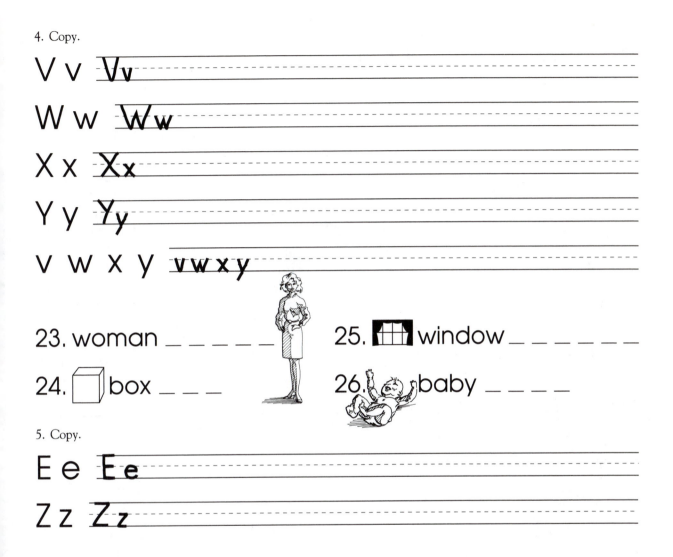

23. woman _ _ _ _ _

24. box _ _ _

25. window _ _ _ _ _ _

26. baby _ _ _ _

5. Copy.

E e   E e _____

Z z   Z z _____

27. envelope _ _ _ _ _ _ _ _

28. umbrella _ _ _ _ _ _ _ _

29. zip code _ _ _   _ _ _ _

30. a black pen _   _ _ _ _ _   _ _ _

31. desk _ _ _ _

32. pencil _ _ _ _ _ _

33. yes _ _ _

6. Copy.

G g *Gg*   J j *Jj*   P p *Pp*

Q q *Qq*   Y y *Yy*

g j p q y *gjpqy*

34. pig _ _ _

35. quarter _ _ _ _ _ _ _

36. eyes _ _ _ _

37. happy _ _ _ _ _

38. jacket _ _ _ _ _ _

7. Copy.

0. zero _ _ _ _   6. six _ _ _

1. one _ _ _   7. seven _ _ _ _ _

2. two _ _ _   8. eight _ _ _ _ _

3. three _ _ _ _ _   9. nine _ _ _ _

4. four _ _ _ _   10. ten _ _ _

5. five _ _ _ _

8. Print your name.

first

last

first   last   first   last

9. Copy the words.

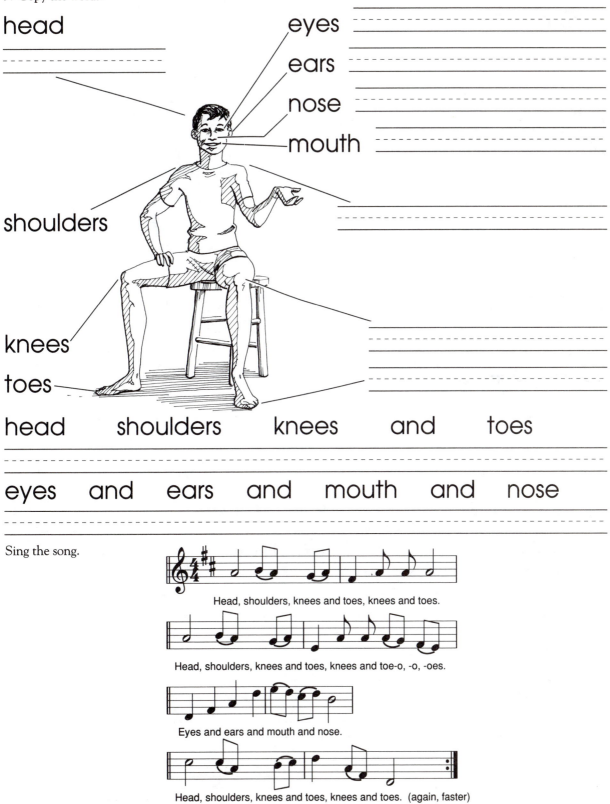

head

eyes

ears

nose

mouth

shoulders

knees

toes

head   shoulders   knees   and   toes

eyes   and   ears   and   mouth   and   nose

Sing the song.

Head, shoulders, knees and toes, knees and toes.

Head, shoulders, knees and toes, knees and toe-o, -o, -oes.

Eyes and ears and mouth and nose.

Head, shoulders, knees and toes, knees and toes. (again, faster)

10. Copy the big (capital) and small letters of the alphabet.

Aa <u>Aa</u> Bb ___ Cc ___ Dd___ Ee ___

Ff ___ Gg___ Hh ___ Ii ___ Jj ___

Kk ___ Ll ___ Mm___ Nn___ Oo ___

Pp ___ Qq___ Rr ___ Ss ___ Tt ___

Uu ___ Vv ___ Ww___ Xx ___ Yy ___ Zz___

11. Print the capital (big) letters.

A B C D E F G H I J K L M N

O P Q R S T U V W X Y Z

12. Print the small letters.

a b c d e f g h i j k l m n

o p q r s t u v w x y z

13. Practice your letters.

14. Read and copy the words.

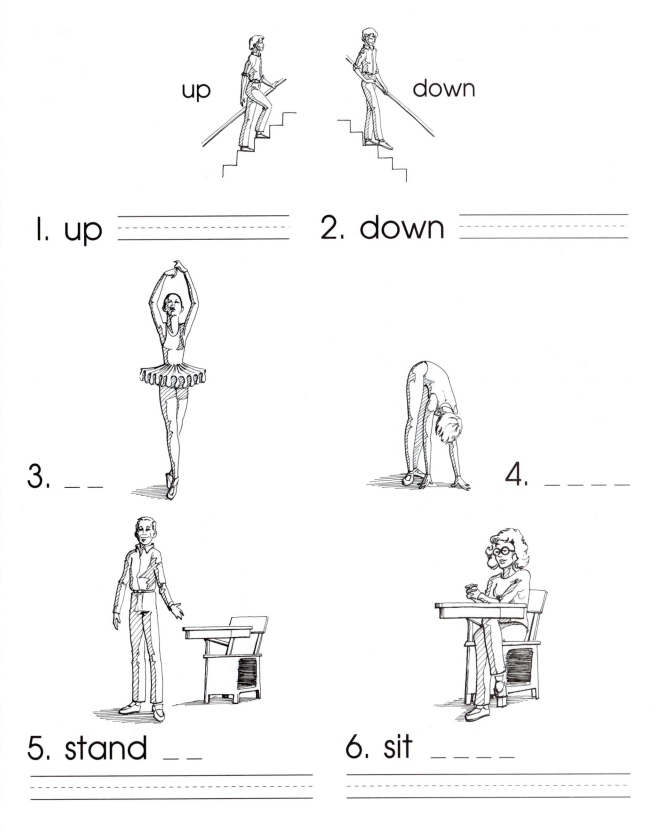

1. up _____

2. down _____

3. _ _

4. _ _ _ _

5. stand _ _
_____

6. sit _ _ _ _ _
_____

15. Read and copy the words.

LEFT
left

RIGHT
right

1. LEFT _____

2. RIGHT _____

3. left _____

4. right _____

5. _ _ _ _ _ ear

6. _ _ _ _ _ ear

_____

_____

7. _ _ _ _ _ hand

8. _ _ _ _ _ hand

_____

_____

Lower-Case Letters

16. Circle the same letter.

p	q	p	P	g	d	b	m	w	n	u	z	m	M
a	o	A	c	a	e	q	h	H	d	n	b	p	h
s	s	z	e	s	S	f	f	t	k	f	f	F	t
g	q	g	p	G	y	g	k	K	t	k	R	h	l
n	r	N	m	u	n	h	x	y	x	X	z	w	v
r	u	r	c	h	R	n	c	b	o	a	c	e	C
y	g	j	Y	i	x	y	b	P	h	b	B	p	d
j	y	i	J	j	f	j	d	g	p	q	d	D	b

(p is circled in the first row)

17. Print the small letters.

a b c d _ _ g h _ _ k l _ n _ _ q r _ _ u _ _ x _ _
_ _ c _ e f _ _ i j _ _ m _ o p _ _ s t _ v w _ y z
a _ c _ e _ g _ i _ k _ m _ o _ q _ s _ u _ w _ y _
_ b _ d _ f _ h _ j _ l _ n _ p _ r _ t _ v _ x _ z

_ _

18. Print the small letters.

A a   B _   C _   D _   E _   F _   G _   H _   I _
J _   K _   L _   M _   N _   O _   P _   Q _   R _
S _   T _   U _   V _   W _   X _   Y _   Z _

19. Read, copy, and answer the questions.

What _ _ _ _   name _ _ _ _

first _ _ _ _ _   last _ _ _ _

is _ _   your _ _ _ _

1. What is your first name?
2. My _ _ _ _ _ name is _____.
3. What _ _ your last _ _ _ _?
4. M_ _ _ _ _ name is _____.
5. Name: _____
   first   middle   last

6. Name: _____
   last   first   middle

Sunday _ _ _ _ _ _   Monday _ _ _ _ _ _

Tuesday _ _ _ _ _ _ _   Wednesday _ _ _ _ _ _ _ _ _

Thursday _ _ _ _ _ _ _ _   Friday _ _ _ _ _ _

Saturday _ _ _ _ _ _ _ _   today _ _ _ _ _

tomorrow _ _ _ _ _ _ _ _   day _ _ _

yesterday _ _ _ _ _ _ _ _ _ was _ _ _

7. What day is today?
8. T_ _ _ _ _ _ _ _____.
9. What day is tomorrow?
10. T_ _ _ _ _ _ _ _ _ _ _ _____.
11. What day was yesterday?
12. Y_ _ _ _ _ _ _ _ _ _ _ _____.

the _ _ _   date _ _ _ _

months _ _ _ _ _ _   July _ _ _ _

January _ _ _ _ _ _ _   August _ _ _ _ _ _

February _ _ _ _ _ _ _ _   September _ _ _ _ _ _ _ _ _

March _ _ _ _ _   October _ _ _ _ _ _ _

April _ _ _ _ _   November _ _ _ _ _ _ _ _

May _ _ _   December _ _ _ _ _ _ _ _

June _ _ _ _

13. What is the date?

14. _____ _ , 19_ _

language _ _ _ _ _ _ _ _   do _ _

you _ _ _   I _   speak _ _ _ _ _

15. What language do you speak?

16. I _ _ _ _ _ _____.

birthdate _ _ _ _ _ _ _ _ _

date of birth _ _ _ _ _ _ _ _ _ _ _ _

17. What is your date of birth?

18. _____ _ , 19_ _

old _ _ _   How _ _ _

years _ _ _ _ _   I _ am _ _

19. How old are you?

20. _ _ _ _ years _ _ _.

He _ _   She _ _ _   is _ _

21. How old is he?
22. H_ _ _ 23 years _ _ _ .
23. How old is she?
24. S _ _ _ _ 40 _ _ _ _ _ old.

Good _ _ _ _   morning _ _ _ _ _ _ _

night _ _ _ _ _   afternoon _ _ _ _ _ _ _ _ _

evening _ _ _ _ _ _ _   How _ _ _

are _ _ _   you _ _ _

Fine _ _ _ _   thank _ _ _ _ _

25. How are you?
26. _ _ _ _ , _ _ _ _ _ _ _ _ .

a _   telephone _ _ _ _ _ _ _ _ _   phone _ _ _ _ _
don't _ _ _ '_   have _ _ _ _

27. What is your telephone number?
28. My p_ _ _ _ n_ _ _ _ _ _ _ □□□-□□□□ .

country _ _ _ _ _ _ _   from _ _ _ _

29. What country are you from?
30. _ _ _ _ _ _ _ _ _____ .

city _ _ _ _   live _ _ _ _   in _ _

state _ _ _ _ _

31. What city do you live in?
32. _ live in _____ .
city

33. What state do you live in?
34. _ _ _ _ _ _ _ _____ .
state

address _ _ _ _ _ _ _   number _ _ _ _ _ _

zip code _ _ _ _ _ _ _   street _ _ _ _ _ _

35. What is your address?
36. My address is _____
number   street   apt. #

_____
city   state   zip code

weekend _ _ _ _ _ _ _   day _ _ _

Have _ _ _ _   nice _ _ _ _

See _ _ _   Good-bye _ _ _ _-_ _ _

You _ _ _   too _ _ _

37. A. Bye. Have a nice d__. A

38. B. Thank _ _ _ . You, too.   B

Read.

A. Good-bye.
B. Bye. Have a nice weekend.
A. Thank you. You too.
B. S_ _ y_ _ M_ _ _ _ _ _ .

A B C D E F G H I J K L M N O P Q R S T U V W X Y Z

20. PRINT IN **CAPITAL** (BIG) LETTERS.

NAME: _____
          FIRST   LAST

ADDRESS: _____
            NUMBER   STREET   APT. #

_____
CITY   STATE   ZIP CODE

DATE: _____
          MONTH   DAY   YEAR

—————————————————————————————————————

a b c d e f g h i j k l m n o p q r s t u v w x y z

21. Print in **small** letters.

Name: _____
         first   last

Address: _____
           number   street   apt. #

_____
city   state   zip code

Date: _____
         month   day   year

What time is it?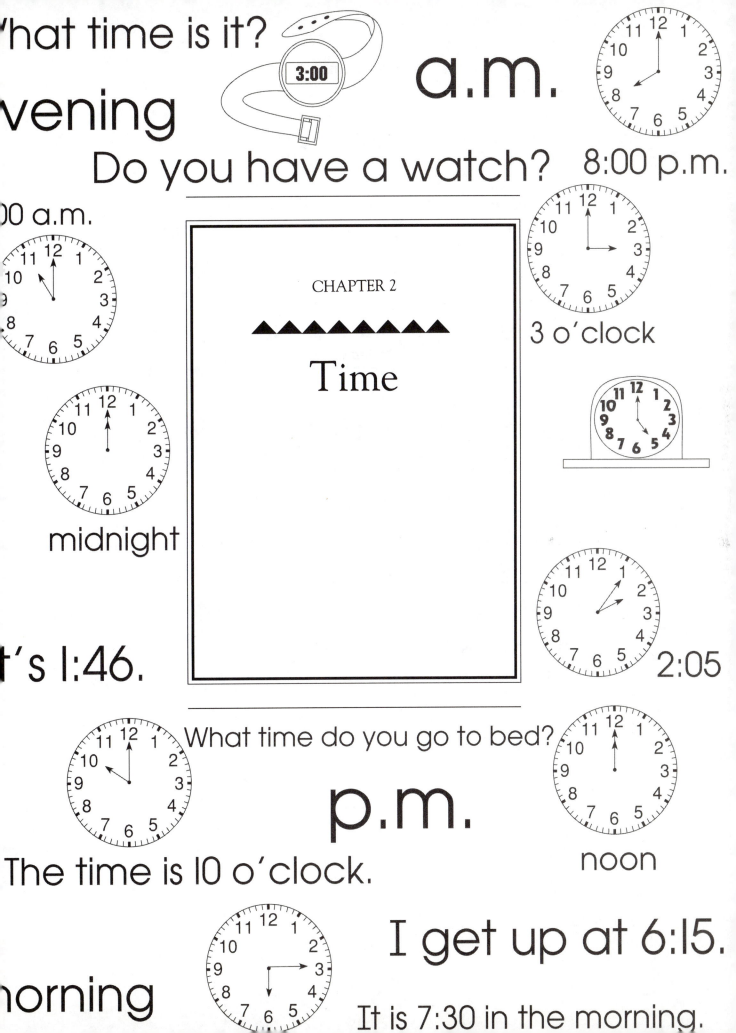

Evening

Do you have a watch?

a.m.

8:00 p.m.

3 o'clock

CHAPTER 2

▲▲▲▲▲▲▲▲

Time

00 a.m.

midnight

It's 1:46.

2:05

What time do you go to bed?

p.m.

noon

The time is 10 o'clock.

I get up at 6:15.

morning

It is 7:30 in the morning.

What time is it?

1.

A. Write the number.

1 **2** 3 4 ___ 6 ___ 8 ___ 10
11 ___ ___ 14 ___ ___ 17 ___ ___ 20
___ 22 ___ ___ 25 ___ 27 ___ 29 ___
31 32 ___ ___ ___ 36 ___ 38 ___ ___
41 ___ ___ 44 ___ ___ 47 ___ ___ 50
___ ___ 53 ___ 55 ___ ___ 58 ___ 60

B. Count by 5's.

5 ___ 15 20 ___ 30 ___ 40 45 ___ ___ 60

C. Count by 10's.

10 20 ___ 40 50 ___

D. Count by 15's.

15 30 ___ 60

E. Write the words.

1. What _ _ _ _ is it?   3. What time is _ _ ?

2. _ _ _ _ time is it?   4. _ _ _ _ _ _ _ _ _ _ _ _ ?

F. Write the minutes.

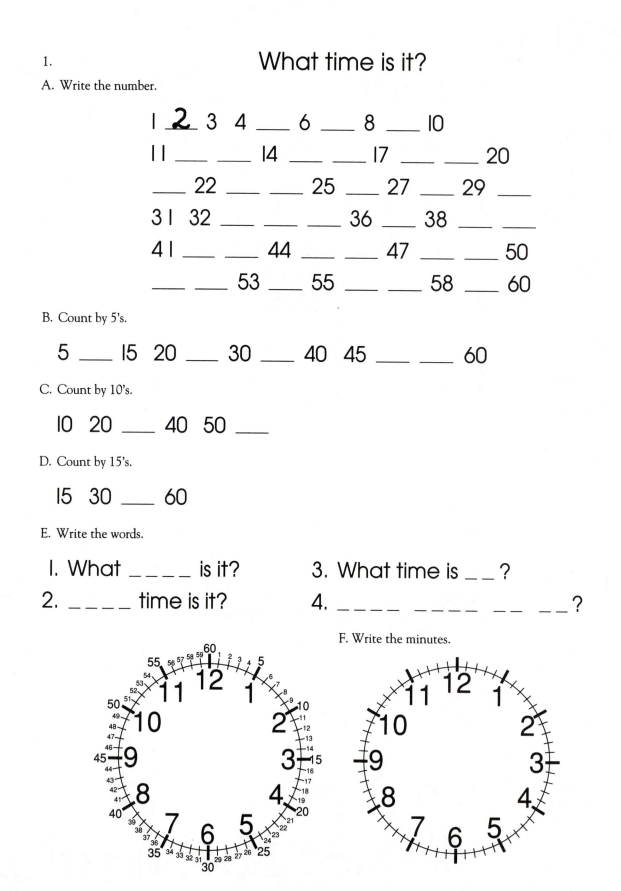

Time

2. Copy.

o'clock
_ _' _ _ _ _ _

Write the numbers.

1 one _ _ _ _
2 two _ _ _ _
3 three _ _ _ _ _ _
4 four _ _ _ _ _
5 five _ _ _ _ _
6 six _ _ _

7 seven _ _ _ _ _ _
8 eight _ _ _ _ _ _
9 nine _ _ _ _ _
10 ten _ _ _ _
11 eleven _ _ _ _ _ _ _
12 twelve _ _ _ _ _ _

3. Write the time.

1. 10:00
   _ _ _

2. 10 o'clock
   _ _' _ _ _ _ _ _ _

3. ten o'clock
   _ _ _' _ _ _ _ _ _

4. _ _ _ _ _

5. _ _ _ _ _

6. _ _ _ _ _

7. _ _ _ _ _

8. _ _ _ _ _

9. 5 o'clock _ _ _ : _ _ _
10. nine o'clock _ _ _ : _ _ _
11. 7 o'clock _ _ _ : _ _ _
12. 1 o'clock _ _ _ : _ _ _
13. four o'clock _ _ _ : _ _ _

STOP Write the time your teacher shows you.

14. _ _ _ : _ _ _
15. _ _ _ : _ _ _
16. _ _ _ : _ _ _
17. _ _ _ : _ _ _
18. _ _ _ : _ _ _
19. _ _ _ : _ _ _

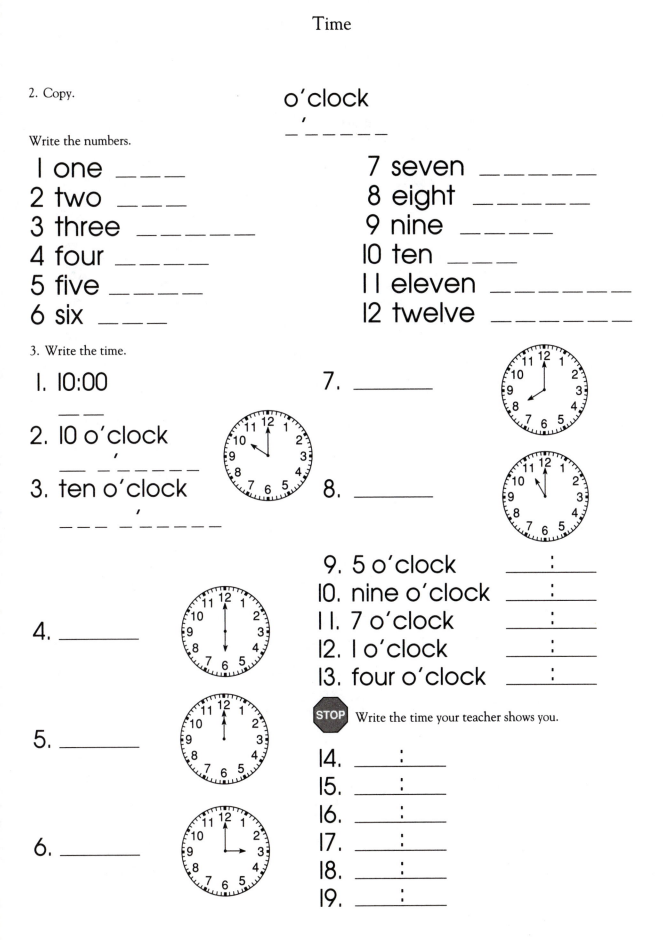

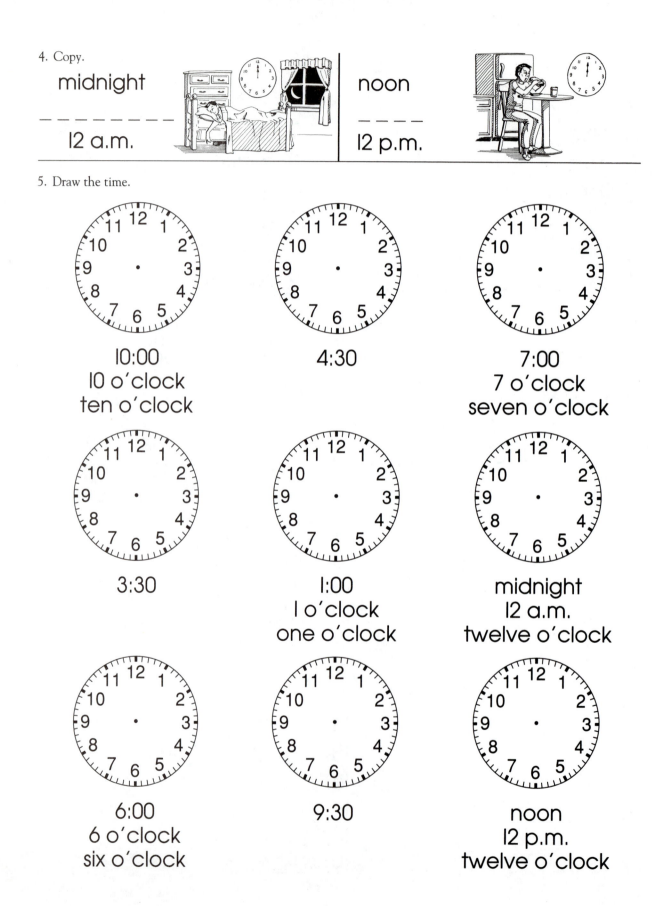

4. Copy.

midnight

– – – – – – –

12 a.m.

noon

– – – –

12 p.m.

5. Draw the time.

10:00
10 o'clock
ten o'clock

4:30

7:00
7 o'clock
seven o'clock

3:30

1:00
1 o'clock
one o'clock

midnight
12 a.m.
twelve o'clock

6:00
6 o'clock
six o'clock

9:30

noon
12 p.m.
twelve o'clock

Time

6. Write these times under the clocks.

6:05	7:00	7:30	9:15	4:45	1:25
3:20	10:50	2:05	9:55	12:30	5:40
8:10	11:35	midnight		noon	

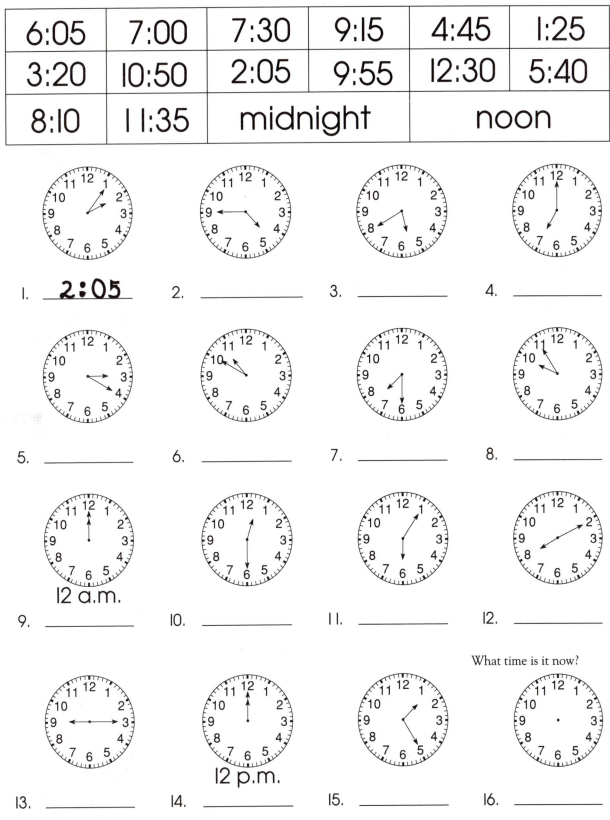

1. **2:05**   2. _____   3. _____   4. _____

5. _____   6. _____   7. _____   8. _____

12 a.m.

9. _____   10. _____   11. _____   12. _____

What time is it now?

12 p.m.

13. _____   14. _____   15. _____   16. _____

7. Write the words.

I. 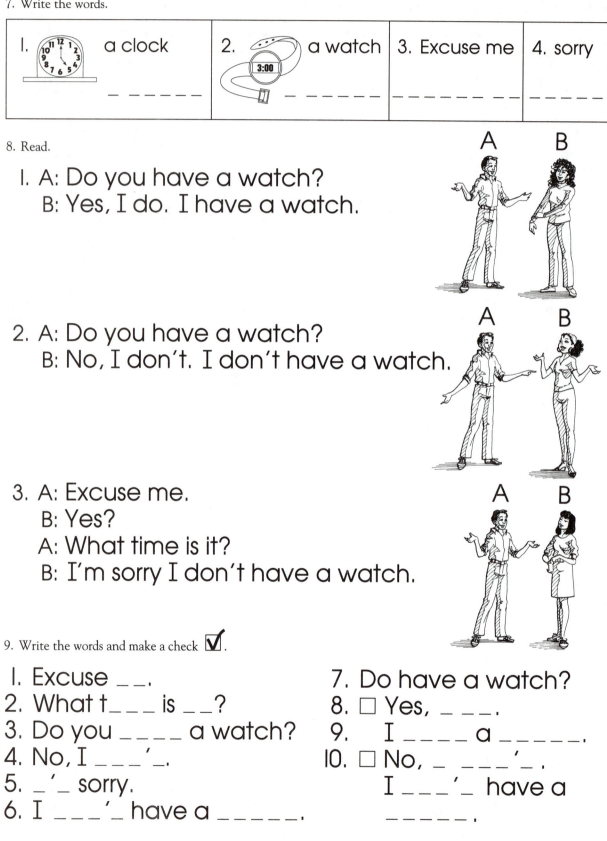 a clock	2. a watch	3. Excuse me	4. sorry
_ _ _ _ _ _	_ _ _ _ _ _	_ _ _ _ _ _ _ _	_ _ _ _ _

8. Read.

I. A: Do you have a watch?
   B: Yes, I do. I have a watch.

A   B

2. A: Do you have a watch?
   B: No, I don't. I don't have a watch.

A   B

3. A: Excuse me.
   B: Yes?
   A: What time is it?
   B: I'm sorry I don't have a watch.

A   B

9. Write the words and make a check ✓.

I. Excuse _ _.
2. What t _ _ _ is _ _?
3. Do you _ _ _ _ a watch?
4. No, I _ _ _ '_.
5. _ '_ sorry.
6. I _ _ _ '_ have a _ _ _ _ _ _.

7. Do have a watch?
8. ☐ Yes, _ _ _ _.
9. I _ _ _ _ a _ _ _ _ _.
10. ☐ No, _ _ _ _ '_.
    I _ _ _ '_ have a
    _ _ _ _ _.

Time

10. Write the words and make a check ☑.

midnight
1. _ _ _ _ _ _ _ _

12 a.m.
2. _ _ _._.

3. What time _ _ _ _?
4. It is 12 m_ _ _ _ _ _t.

noon
5. _ _ _ _

6. 12 p.m.
_ _ _._.

7. What _ _ _ _ is _ _?
8. It is 12 n_ _ _.

9. midnight ☐ a.m.   ☐ p.m.
10. noon   ☐ a.m.   ☐ p.m.

11. Write the words.

in the morning	12:01 – 11:59	a.m.
_ _ _ _ _ _ _ _ _ _ _ _		_._.
in the afternoon	12:01 – 5:59	p.m.
_ _ _ _ _ _ _ _ _ _ _ _		_._.
in the evening	6:00 – 8:59	p.m.
_ _ _ _ _ _ _ _ _		_._.
at night	9:00 – 11:59	p.m.
_ _ _ _ _ _ _		_._.

12. Make a check ☑.

1. 11 a.m.   ☑ in the morning ☐ in the afternoon ☐ in the evening ☐ at night
2. 3:30 a.m. ☐ in the morning ☐ in the afternoon ☐ in the evening ☐ at night
3. 10:15 p.m. ☐ in the morning ☐ in the afternoon ☐ in the evening ☐ at night
4. 6 p.m.   ☐ in the morning ☐ in the afternoon ☐ in the evening ☐ at night
5. 6 a.m.   ☐ in the morning ☐ in the afternoon ☐ in the evening ☐ at night
6. 11:45 p.m. ☐ in the morning ☐ in the afternoon ☐ in the evening ☐ at night
7. 4:30 p.m. ☐ in the morning ☐ in the afternoon ☐ in the evening ☐ at night
8. 2:00 a.m. ☐ in the morning ☐ in the afternoon ☐ in the evening ☐ at night
9. 8:15 p.m. ☐ in the morning ☐ in the afternoon ☐ in the evening ☐ at night
10. 1:45 p.m. ☐ in the morning ☐ in the afternoon ☐ in the evening ☐ at night

13. Read.

I. A: What time do you **get up** in the morning?

Draw the time.

I.

B: I **get up** at 6:30 in the morning.

2. A: What time do you **go to bed** at night?

2.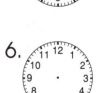

B: I **go to bed** at midnight.

3. A: What time do you **come to school**?

3.

B: I **come to school** at 6:00 in the evening.

14. Write the answers to the questions.

Draw the time.

I. What time do you **get up** in the morning?

2. I _ _ _ _ _ at _____.

3.

4. What time do you **go to bed** at night?

5. I _ _ _ _ _ _ _ at _____.

6.

7. What time do you **come to school**?

8. I _ _ _ _ _ _ _ _ _ _ _ _ at _____.

9.

15. Read.   Draw the time.

I. A: What time is your **class**?
   B: My **class** is at 8:30.

2. A: What time do you **go to work**?
   B: I don't work.

3. A: What time do you **go home**?
   B: I **go home** at I:00.

16. Write the words, and make a check ☑.

1. What time is your **class**?
2. ☐ I have one **class**.
   My **c**_ _ _ _ is at _____.

   ☐ I have 2 classes.
   ☐ I have 3 classes.
   My first class is at _____.
   My second class is at _____.
   My third class is at _____.

3. What time do you **go to work**?
4. ☐ I __ __ ____ at _____.
   ☐ I don't ____.

5. What time do you **go home**?
6. ☐ I __ ____ from work at _____.
7. ☐ I __ ____ from school at _____.

8. What time is it **now**?
9. It's _____.

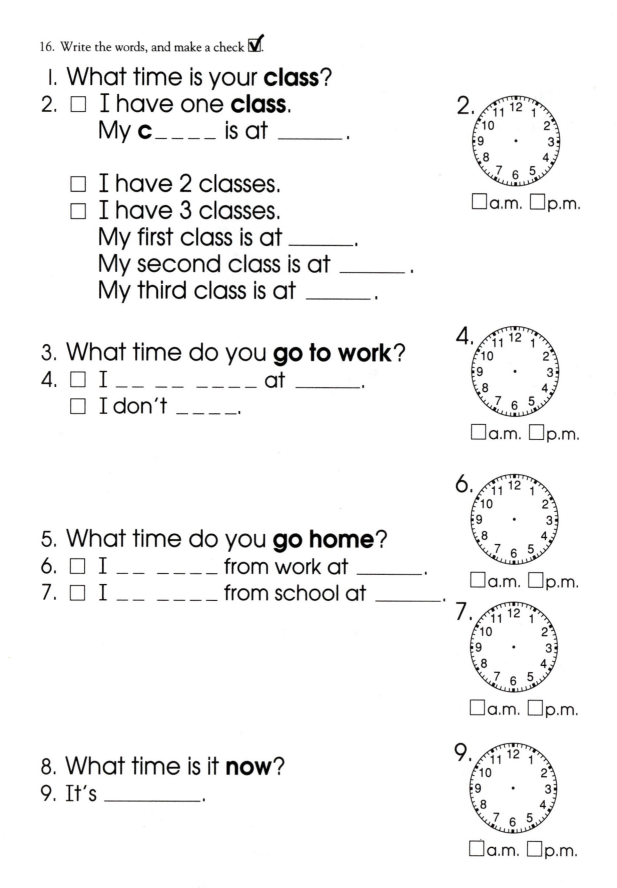

2. ☐ a.m. ☐ p.m.

4. ☐ a.m. ☐ p.m.

6. ☐ a.m. ☐ p.m.

7. ☐ a.m. ☐ p.m.

9. ☐ a.m. ☐ p.m.

17. Write the words.

eat	breakfast
I. _ _ _	2. _ _ _ _ _ _ _ _ _
	lunch
	3. _ _ _ _ _
	dinner
	4. _ _ _ _ _ _

18. Read.

I. A: What time do you **eat breakfast**?
   B: I **eat breakfast** at 7:00.

2. A: What time do you **eat lunch**?
   B: I **eat lunch** at noon.

3. A: What time do you **eat dinner**?
   B: I **eat dinner** at 6:00 in the evening.

Draw the time.

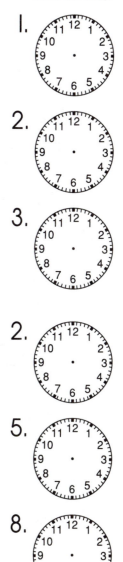

19. Write the words and make a check ✓ .

I. What time do you **eat breakfast**?
2. ☐ I _ _ _ _ _ _ _ _ _ _ _ _ at _ _ _ _ _ _ .
3. ☐ I don't _ _ _ _ _ _ _ _ _ _ _ _ .

4. What time do you **eat lunch**?
5. ☐ I _ _ _ _ _ _ _ _ at _ _ _ _ _ _ .
6. ☐ I don't _ _ _ _ _ _ _ _ .

7. What time do you **eat dinner**?
8. I _ _ _ _ _ _ _ _ _ _ _ _ _ _ _ _ _ _ .

20. Write the words and make a check ☑; then, stand up and tell the class.

My Day

I. _ _   _ _ _

2. My name is _____ .
   FIRST   LAST

3. I get up at _____.

4. ☐ I eat breakfast at _____.
   ☐ I don't eat breakfast.

5. ☐ I eat lunch at _____.
   ☐ I don't eat lunch.

6. I come to school at _____ .
   ☐ I have one class. My class is at _____.

   ☐ I have _____ classes. My first class is at _____ and
           #   my second class is at ____.

7. ☐ I go to work at _____   ☐ a.m.
                               ☐ p.m.

   ☐ I don't work.

8. I go home at _____ ☐ a.m.
                _____ ☐ p.m.

9. I eat dinner at _____, and
10. I go to bed at _____ .

21. Write the words.

appointment

I. _ _ _ _ _ _ _ _ _ _ _

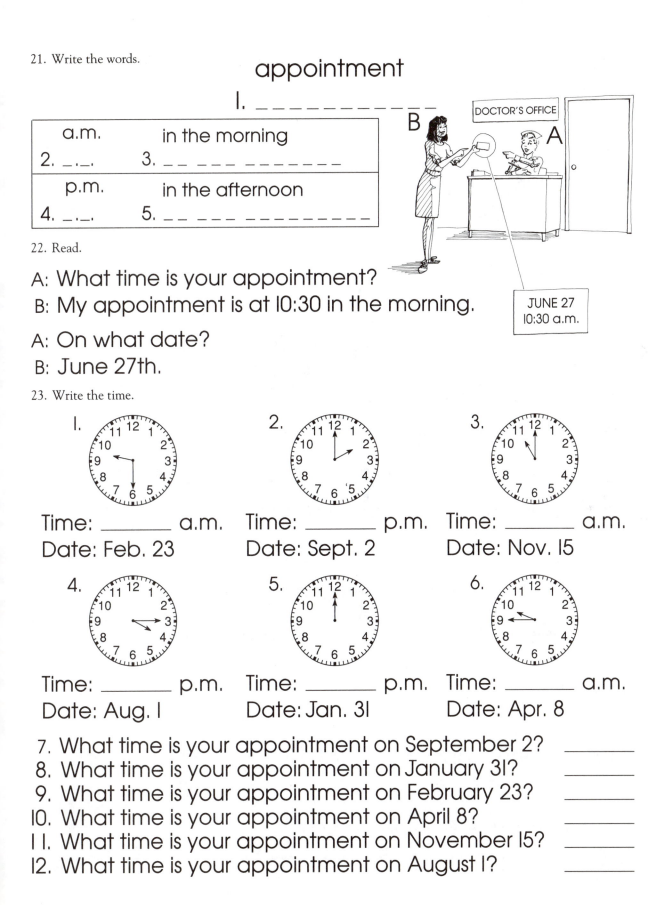

a.m.	in the morning
2. _._.	3. _ _ _ _ _ _ _ _ _ _ _
p.m.	in the afternoon
4. _._.	5. _ _ _ _ _ _ _ _ _ _ _

DOCTOR'S OFFICE

B   A

JUNE 27
10:30 a.m.

22. Read.

A: What time is your appointment?

B: My appointment is at 10:30 in the morning.

A: On what date?

B: June 27th.

23. Write the time.

I.

Time: _____ a.m.
Date: Feb. 23

2.

Time: _____ p.m.
Date: Sept. 2

3.

Time: _____ a.m.
Date: Nov. 15

4.

Time: _____ p.m.
Date: Aug. 1

5.

Time: _____ p.m.
Date: Jan. 31

6.

Time: _____ a.m.
Date: Apr. 8

7. What time is your appointment on September 2? _____

8. What time is your appointment on January 31? _____

9. What time is your appointment on February 23? _____

10. What time is your appointment on April 8? _____

11. What time is your appointment on November 15? _____

12. What time is your appointment on August 1? _____

24. Read.

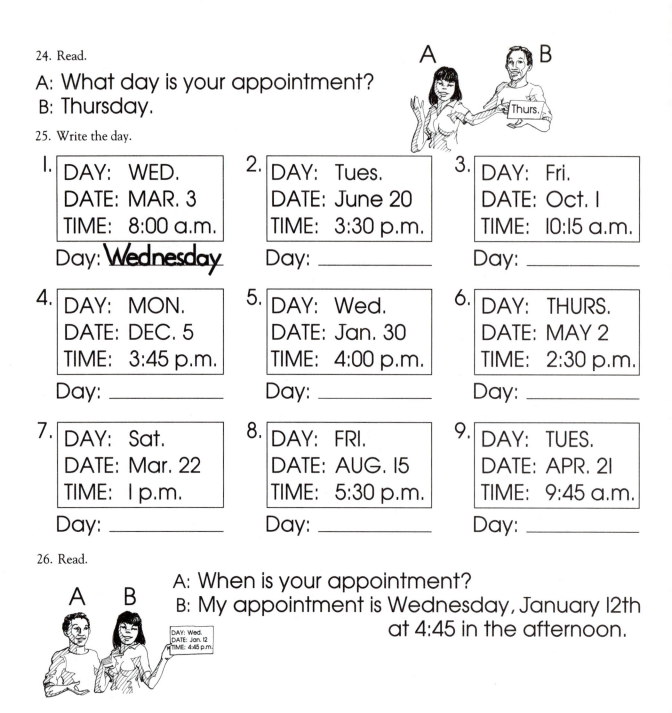

A: What day is your appointment?
B: Thursday.

25. Write the day.

1.
DAY: WED.
DATE: MAR. 3
TIME: 8:00 a.m.

Day: **Wednesday**

2.
DAY: Tues.
DATE: June 20
TIME: 3:30 p.m.

Day: _____

3.
DAY: Fri.
DATE: Oct. 1
TIME: 10:15 a.m.

Day: _____

4.
DAY: MON.
DATE: DEC. 5
TIME: 3:45 p.m.

Day: _____

5.
DAY: Wed.
DATE: Jan. 30
TIME: 4:00 p.m.

Day: _____

6.
DAY: THURS.
DATE: MAY 2
TIME: 2:30 p.m.

Day: _____

7.
DAY: Sat.
DATE: Mar. 22
TIME: 1 p.m.

Day: _____

8.
DAY: FRI.
DATE: AUG. 15
TIME: 5:30 p.m.

Day: _____

9.
DAY: TUES.
DATE: APR. 21
TIME: 9:45 a.m.

Day: _____

26. Read.

A: When is your appointment?
B: My appointment is Wednesday, January 12th
     at 4:45 in the afternoon.

DAY: Wed.
DATE: Jan. 12
TIME: 4:45 p.m.

Look at the cards in Exercise 25.

1. When is your appointment (#3)?
2. My appointment is _____ , _____ __ , **a t** _____ .
                            DAY   DATE   TIME
3. When is your appointment (#7)?
4. My _ _ _ _ _ _ _ _ _ _ _ is _____ , _____ __ , __ _____ .
                                    DAY   DATE   TIME

30

27. Copy the words.

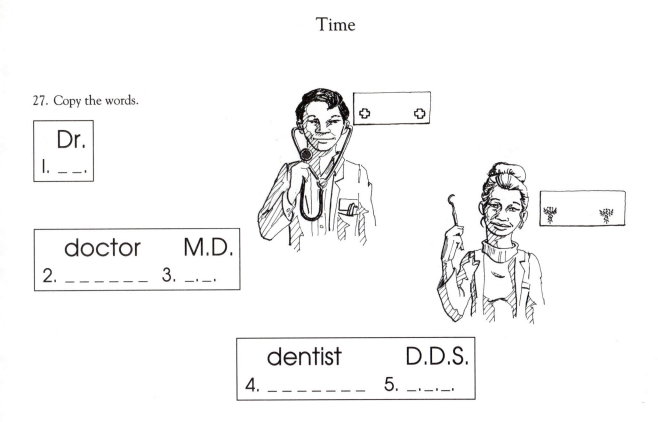

Dr.
1. _ _.

doctor   M.D.
2. _ _ _ _ _ _   3. _._.

dentist   D.D.S.
4. _ _ _ _ _ _ _   5. _._._.

6. When is your appointment?

7. My appointment is _____, _____ at _____.
                          DAY   DATE   TIME

28. Read the appointment cards and write the DAY, DATE, and TIME.

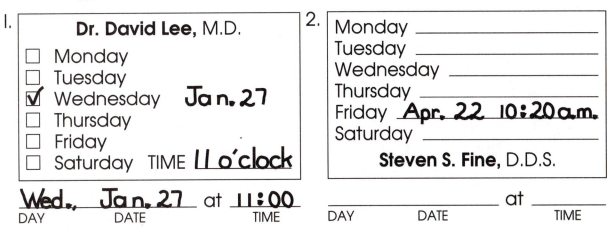

1.
Dr. David Lee, M.D.
☐ Monday
☐ Tuesday
☑ Wednesday   Jan. 27
☐ Thursday
☐ Friday
☐ Saturday   TIME II o'clock

Wed., Jan. 27 at **II:00**
DAY   DATE   TIME

2.
Monday _____
Tuesday _____
Wednesday _____
Thursday _____
Friday Apr. 22 10:20 a.m.
Saturday _____
Steven S. Fine, D.D.S.

_____ at _____
DAY   DATE   TIME

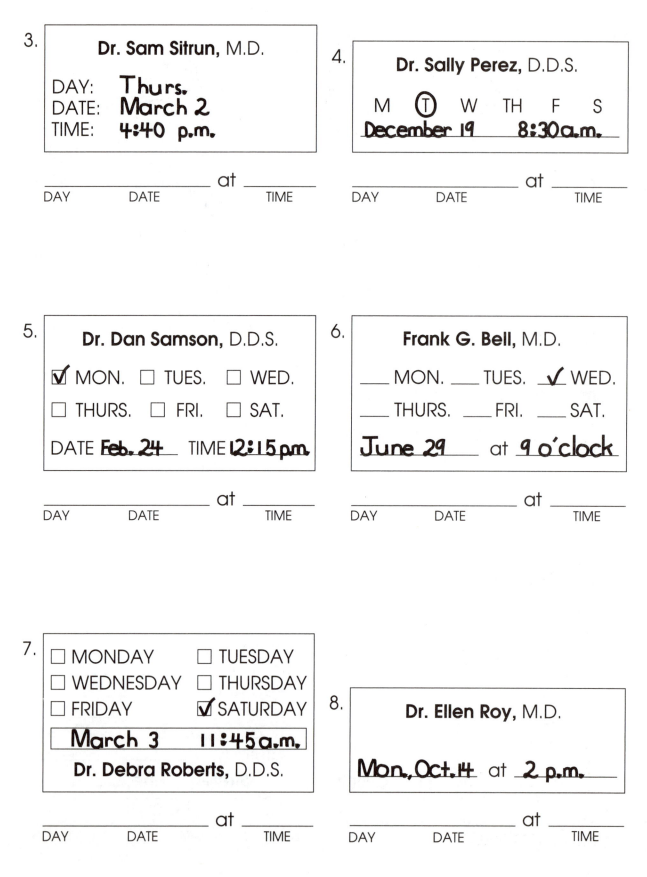

3.

Dr. Sam Sitrun, M.D.

DAY: Thurs.
DATE: March 2
TIME: 4:40 p.m.

_____ at _____
DAY   DATE   TIME

4.

Dr. Sally Perez, D.D.S.

M (T) W TH F S
December 19   8:30 a.m.

_____ at _____
DAY   DATE   TIME

5.

Dr. Dan Samson, D.D.S.

☑ MON. ☐ TUES. ☐ WED.
☐ THURS. ☐ FRI. ☐ SAT.

DATE Feb. 24   TIME 12:15 pm

_____ at _____
DAY   DATE   TIME

6.

Frank G. Bell, M.D.

___ MON. ___ TUES. ✓ WED.
___ THURS. ___ FRI. ___ SAT.

June 29   at 9 o'clock

_____ at _____
DAY   DATE   TIME

7.

☐ MONDAY   ☐ TUESDAY
☐ WEDNESDAY   ☐ THURSDAY
☐ FRIDAY   ☑ SATURDAY
March 3   11:45 a.m.
Dr. Debra Roberts, D.D.S.

_____ at _____
DAY   DATE   TIME

8.

Dr. Ellen Roy, M.D.

Mon., Oct. 14 at 2 p.m.

_____ at _____
DAY   DATE   TIME

Read and copy.

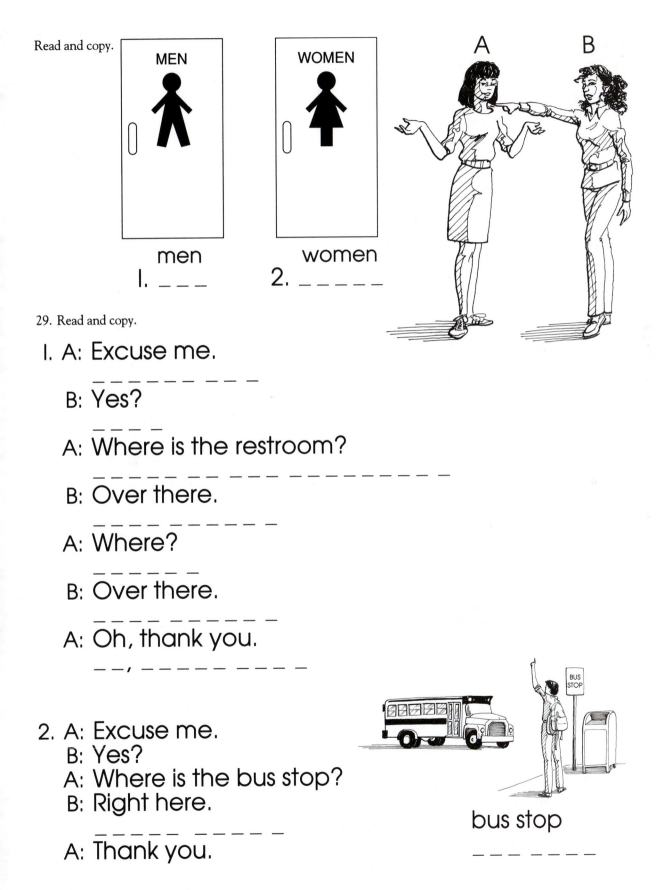

MEN

men

1. _ _ _

WOMEN

women

2. _ _ _ _ _

A   B

29. Read and copy.

1. A: Excuse me.

_ _ _ _ _ _ _ _ _

B: Yes?

_ _ _ _

A: Where is the restroom?

_ _ _ _ _ _ _ _ _ _ _ _ _ _ _ _ _ _ _

B: Over there.

_ _ _ _ _ _ _ _ _ _

A: Where?

_ _ _ _ _ _ _

B: Over there.

_ _ _ _ _ _ _ _ _ _ _

A: Oh, thank you.

_ _ , _ _ _ _ _ _ _ _ _

2. A: Excuse me.
   B: Yes?
   A: Where is the bus stop?
   B: Right here.

_ _ _ _ _ _ _ _ _ _

   A: Thank you.

bus stop

_ _ _ _ _ _ _

30. Read and copy.

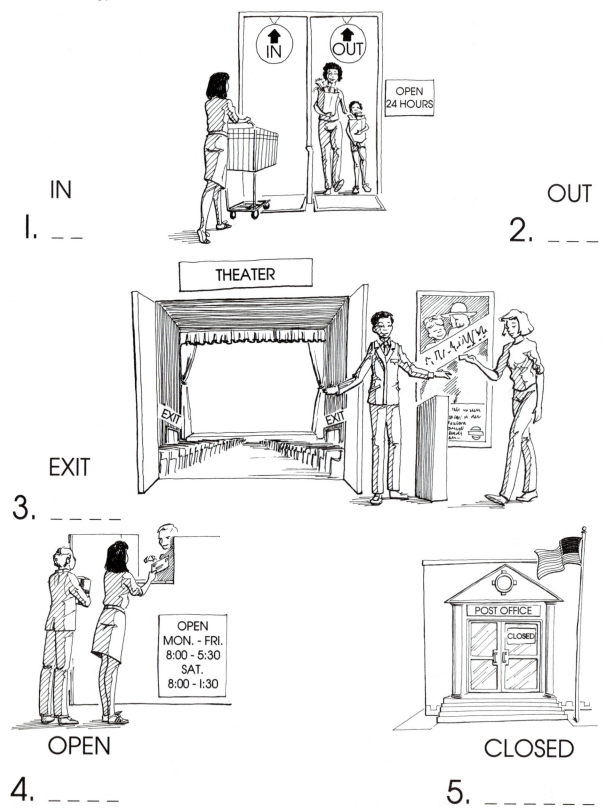

IN

1. _ _

OUT

2. _ _ _ _

EXIT

3. _ _ _ _ _

OPEN

4. _ _ _ _ _

CLOSED

5. _ _ _ _ _ _

31. Read and copy the words.

en

1.  pen ---------------------------------

2. ten --

3. men --

4. When ----------------------------------

DOCTOR'S OFFICE

When is your appointment?

Wed., Sept. 7th
10:00

| **en** | pen | ten | men | When |

STOP Write the sentences your teacher says.

1. _____

2. _____

3. _____

35

A nickel is 5¢.

$100.00

Count your dimes.

25¢

DOLLARS

$20.00

13¢

CHAPTER 3

▲▲▲▲▲▲▲▲

Money

How much is this?

CENTS

$.05

1¢

ow many pennies are in a dollar?

10¢

$.50

1. Copy the words.

Write how much.

a. money

_ _ _ _ _

b. dollars _ _ _ _ _ _ _

c. $ __

d. cents _ _ _ _ _

e. ¢ __

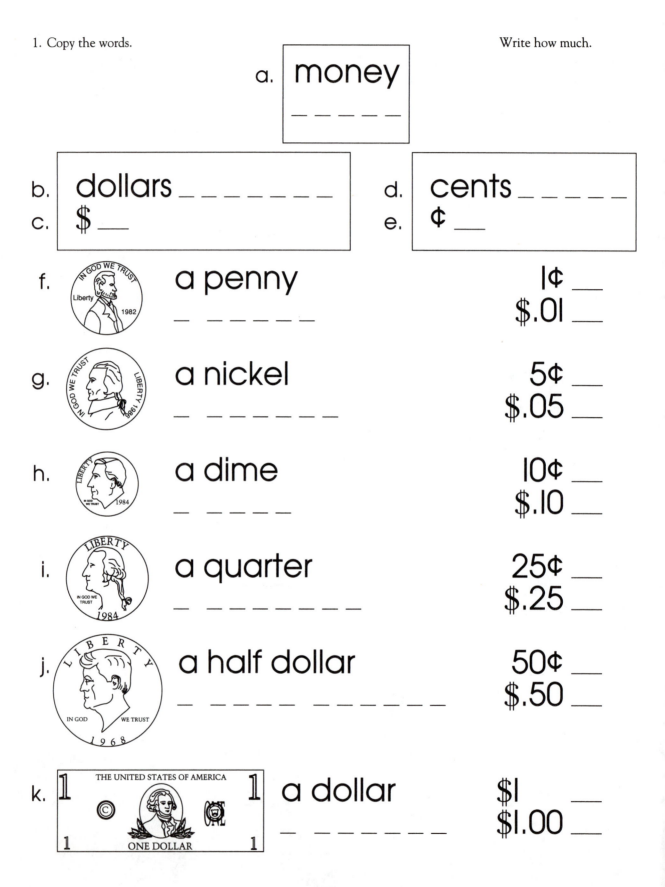

f. a penny

_ _ _ _ _ _

1¢ __

$.01 __

g. a nickel

_ _ _ _ _ _ _

5¢ __

$.05 __

h. a dime

_ _ _ _ _

10¢ __

$.10 __

i. a quarter

_ _ _ _ _ _ _ _

25¢ __

$.25 __

j. a half dollar

_ _ _ _ _ _ _ _ _ _

50¢ __

$.50 __

k. a dollar

_ _ _ _ _ _ _

$1 __

$1.00 __

Money

2. Count your pennies.

A. Write the words and numbers.

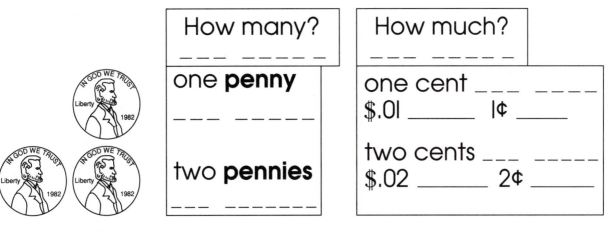

How many?	How much?
___ _____ _	___ _____ _
one **penny**	one cent ___ _____
___ _____	$.01 _____ 1¢ _____
two **pennies**	two cents ___ _____
___ _____	$.02 _____ 2¢ _____

B. Write how much.

1¢	2¢	___	4¢	___	6¢	7¢	___	9¢	10¢
11¢	___	13¢	___	15¢	___	___	18¢	___	20¢
___	22¢	___	___	25¢	26¢	___	___	29¢	___
31¢	___	___	___	___	36¢	37¢	___	___	___
41¢	42¢	___	___	45¢	___	47¢	48¢	___	___
51¢	___	___	___	55¢	___	___	___	59¢	60¢
___	___	63¢	64¢	___	___	67¢	___	69¢	___
71¢	___	___	___	75¢	___	___	78¢	___	___
81¢	___	___	___	86¢	___	___	___	___	___
___	92¢	___	___	___	___	___	___	___	$1

C. Read and copy.

How much is this?

1. ___ _____ __ _____ _

one dollar

2. ___ _____

3. $1.00 _____ . _____

4. $1 _____

5. How many pennies are in $1? [   ] pennies

39

3. Count your nickels.

   A. Write the words and numbers.

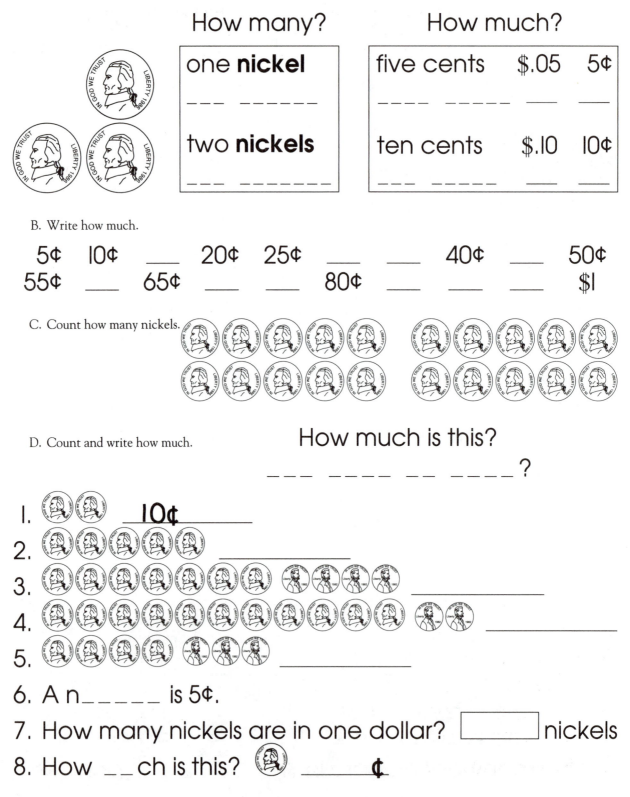

How many?

| one **nickel** |
| _ _ _ _ _ _ _ _ _ _ |
| two **nickels** |
| _ _ _ _ _ _ _ _ _ _ |

How much?

five cents	$.05	5¢
_ _ _ _ _ _ _ _ _	_ _ _	_ _
ten cents	$.10	10¢
_ _ _ _ _ _ _ _	_ _	_ _

   B. Write how much.

   5¢   10¢   ___   20¢   25¢   ___   ___   40¢   ___   50¢
   55¢   ___   65¢   ___   80¢   ___   ___   ___ $1

   C. Count how many nickels.

   D. Count and write how much.

   How much is this?
   _ _ _ _ _ _ _ _ _ _ _ _ _ ?

   1. ___10¢_____
   2. _____
   3. _____
   4. _____
   5. _____
   6. A n_ _ _ _ _ is 5¢.
   7. How many nickels are in one dollar? [____]nickels
   8. How _ _ ch is this? _____ ¢

Money

4. Count your dimes.

A. Write the words and numbers.

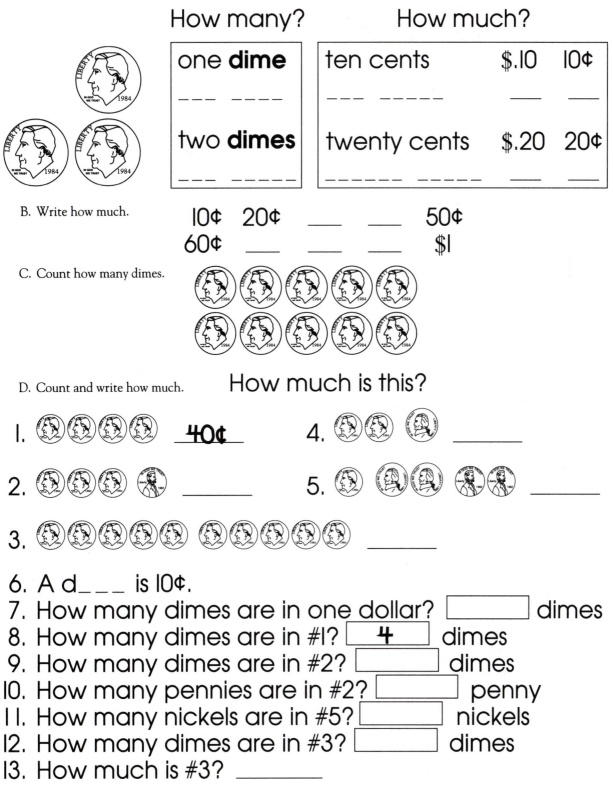

How many?	How much?
one **dime**	ten cents $.10 10¢
___ ____	___ _____ ___ ___
two **dimes**	twenty cents $.20 20¢
___ _____	_____ _____ ___ ___

B. Write how much.

10¢ 20¢ ___ ___ 50¢
60¢ ___ ___ ___ $1

C. Count how many dimes.

D. Count and write how much.

How much is this?

1. __40¢__

4. _____

2. _____

5. _____

3. _____

6. A d_ _ _ is 10¢.
7. How many dimes are in one dollar? [_____] dimes
8. How many dimes are in #1? [__4__] dimes
9. How many dimes are in #2? [_____] dimes
10. How many pennies are in #2? [_____] penny
11. How many nickels are in #5? [_____] nickels
12. How many dimes are in #3? [_____] dimes
13. How much is #3? _____

5. Read.

I. A: Do you have a nickel for five pennies?
   B: Yes, I have a nickel. Here.

   A: Thank you.
   B: You're welcome.

Copy.

   I. Do you have a nickel for five pennies?
   2. __ ___ ____ _ _____ ___ ____
      _____ _
   3. Yes, I have a nickel. Here.
   4. ___, _ ____ _ _____ _ ____ _
   5. Thank you.
   6. _____ ___ .
   7. You're welcome.
   8. ___'__ _____ .

Look at the pictures.

Do you have two nickels for a dime?

Yes. I have two _____.

No. I have a _____ and five _____.

2.

A   B   C

Do you have a dime for ten pennies?

3. A

Yes. I have a _____.

B

Money

6. Count your quarters.

A. Write the words and numbers.

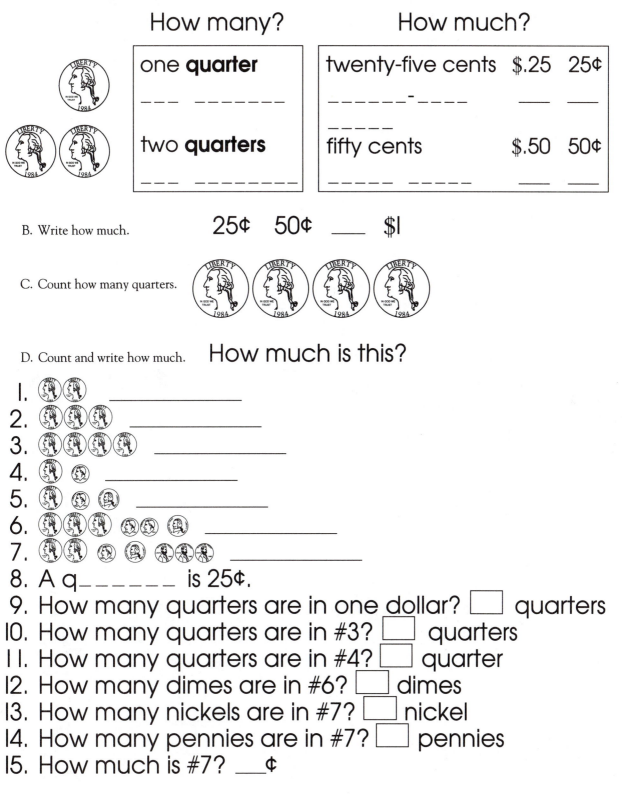

How many?   How much?

one **quarter**	twenty-five cents $.25 25¢
___ _____	_____-____ ___ ___
two **quarters**	fifty cents $.50 50¢
___ _____	_____ _____ ___ ___

B. Write how much.   25¢   50¢   ___ $1

C. Count how many quarters.

D. Count and write how much.   How much is this?

1. _____
2. _____
3. _____
4. _____
5. _____
6. _____
7. _____
8. A q_____ is 25¢.
9. How many quarters are in one dollar? ☐ quarters
10. How many quarters are in #3? ☐ quarters
11. How many quarters are in #4? ☐ quarter
12. How many dimes are in #6? ☐ dimes
13. How many nickels are in #7? ☐ nickel
14. How many pennies are in #7? ☐ pennies
15. How much is #7? ___¢

7. Read and copy the words.

1. A: Do you have change for a dollar?
   B: Sorry. I don't have any money.
   A: Oh. That's OK.

   1. Do you have change for a dollar?
   2. _
      _ _ _ _ _ _ _ _

   3. Sorry. I don't have any money.
   4. _ _ _ _ _ _. _ _ _ _'_ _ _ _ _ _ _ _ _ _
      _ _ _ _ _ _

   5. Oh. That's OK.
   6. _ _. _ _ _ _ _'_ _ _.

Look at the pictures.

2. A: Do you have change for a
      d_ _ _ _ _?
   B: Yes, I have four _ _ _ _ _ _ _ _ _.
      Here.
   A: Thank you.
   B: You're welcome.

3. A: Do you have change for
      a q_ _ _ _ _ _ _?
   B: Yes, I have two _ _ _ _ _ _
      and a _ _ _ _ _ _ _.
      Here.
   A: Thank you.
   B: You're welcome.

Money

8. Count your half dollars.

   A. Write the words and numbers.

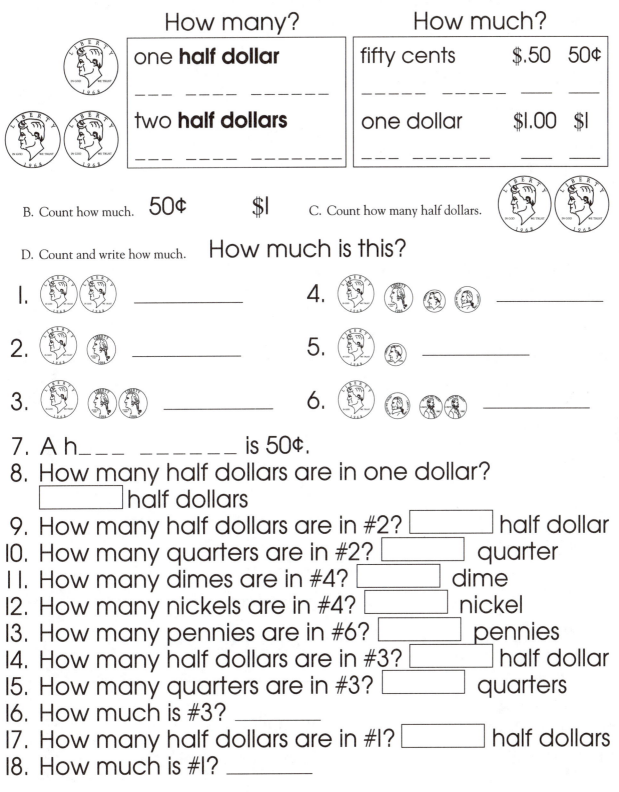

How many?		How much?		
one **half dollar**		fifty cents	$.50	50¢
___ ____ _____		_____ _____ ___ ___		
two **half dollars**		one dollar	$1.00	$1
___ ____ _____		___ _____ ___ ___		

B. Count how much. 50¢ $1   C. Count how many half dollars.

D. Count and write how much. **How much is this?**

1. _____   4. _____

2. _____   5. _____

3. _____   6. _____

7. A h___ _____ is 50¢.
8. How many half dollars are in one dollar?
   [   ] half dollars
9. How many half dollars are in #2? [   ] half dollar
10. How many quarters are in #2? [   ] quarter
11. How many dimes are in #4? [   ] dime
12. How many nickels are in #4? [   ] nickel
13. How many pennies are in #6? [   ] pennies
14. How many half dollars are in #3? [   ] half dollar
15. How many quarters are in #3? [   ] quarters
16. How much is #3? _____
17. How many half dollars are in #1? [   ] half dollars
18. How much is #1? _____

45

9. Read.

A: Please give me five dollars.
B: Here.
A: Thanks.
B: You're welcome.

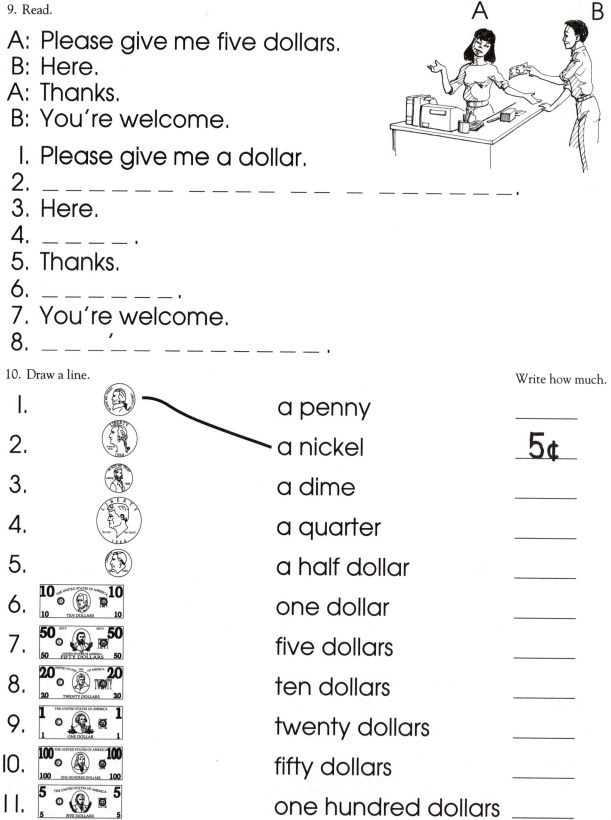

1. Please give me a dollar.
2. _.
3. Here.
4. _ _ _ _ _ _ .
5. Thanks.
6. _ _ _ _ _ _ _ .
7. You're welcome.
8. _ _ _ _ _ ' _ _ _ _ _ _ _ _ _ .

10. Draw a line.   Write how much.

1.		a penny	_____
2.		a nickel	5¢
3.		a dime	_____
4.		a quarter	_____
5.		a half dollar	_____
6.		one dollar	_____
7.		five dollars	_____
8.		ten dollars	_____
9.		twenty dollars	_____
10.		fifty dollars	_____
11.		one hundred dollars	_____

Money

11. Read how much.

1.	30¢	21.	$10.03	41.	$75	61.	$.02
2.	$.30	22.	$10.30	42.	75¢	62.	$18
3.	10¢	23.	$103	43.	$.75	63.	$80
4.	$.10	24.	$.50	44.	$7.50	64.	80¢
5.	$10	25.	50¢	45.	$7.05	65.	$.18
6.	$10.00	26.	$1.50	46.	$70.50	66.	$17.80
7.	$100	27.	$150	47.	$.07	67.	$70.18
8.	5¢	28.	$15	48.	$16	68.	$80.70
9.	$.05	29.	$15.00	49.	$60	69.	$18.17
10.	$2	30.	$1.15	50.	$60.16	70.	$.04
11.	$2.00	31.	$3.50	51.	$16.60	71.	$.40
12.	$20.00	32.	$35.00	52.	$16.16	72.	$40
13.	$200	33.	$350.00	53.	$60.60	73.	$400
14.	$2.34	34.	$35.50	54.	$166.00	74.	$404
15.	$4.85	35.	$355	55.	66¢	75.	$444
16.	$6.92	36.	$.06	56.	25¢	76.	$44
17.	$8.08	37.	$.08	57.	$25	77.	$.44
18.	$8.80	38.	$.09	58.	$205	78.	90¢
19.	$8.18	39.	$9.00	59.	$25.25	79.	$19
20.	$81.00	40.	$90	60.	$252.50	80.	$19.90

STOP 12. Write how much.

1.		5.		9.		13.	
2.		6.		10.		14.	
3.		7.		11.		15.	
4.		8.		12.		16.	

13. Count the money.

How much do you have?

― ― ― ― ― ― ― ― ― ― ― ― ―

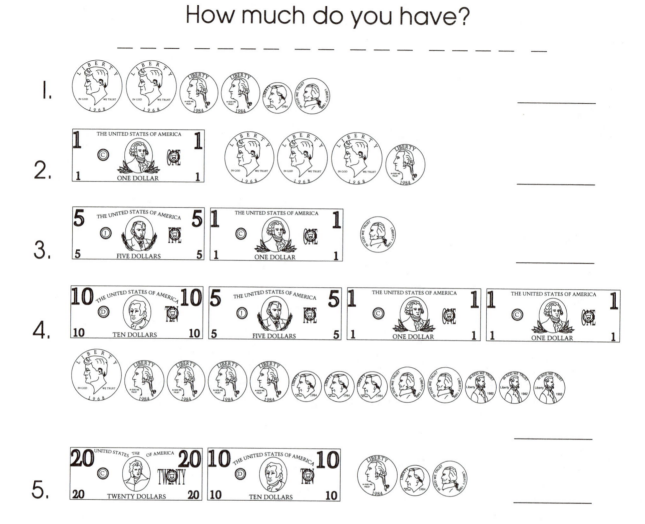

1. _____

2. _____

3. _____

4. _____

_____

5. _____

14. Draw the money.

6. $1.41 | I | 25 10 5 1

7. 79¢

8. $3.64

9. $8.88

10. $16.32

11. $27.93

15. Read.

A: I'm going to the post office.
B: Why?
A: I need a stamp.

Copy.

1. I'm going to the post office.
2. _ _´ _ _ _ _ _ _ _ _ _ _ _ _ _ _ _ _ _ _ _ —.
3. Why?
4. _ _ _ _ _
5. I need a stamp.
6. _ _ _ _ _ _ _ _ _ _ _ _ _ _ _ —.

7.  a stamp
_ _ _ _ _ _

8. two stamps
_ _ _ _ _ _ _ _ _

9. an airmail stamp
_ _ _ _ _ _

_ _ _ _ _

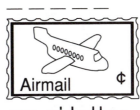

10. a postcard

_ _ _ _ _ _ _ _

11. an airletter

_ _ _ _ _ _ _ _

49

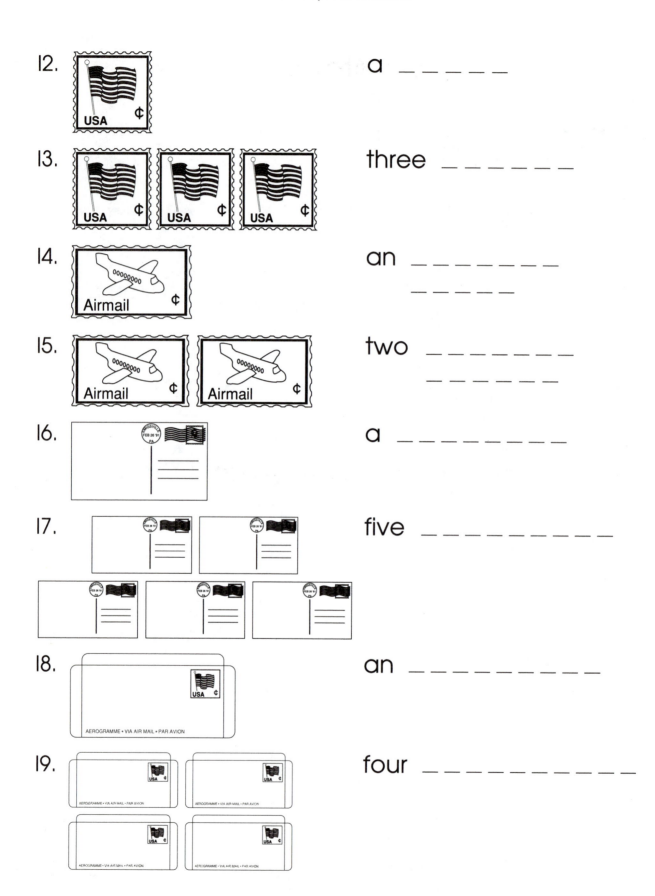

12. a _ _ _ _ _

13. three _ _ _ _ _ _

14. an _ _ _ _ _ _ _
    _ _ _ _ _

15. two _ _ _ _ _ _
    _ _ _ _ _

16. a _ _ _ _ _ _ _ _

17. five _ _ _ _ _ _ _ _ _

18. an _ _ _ _ _ _ _ _ _ _

19. four _ _ _ _ _ _ _ _ _ _ _

20. How much is a stamp? _____ ¢

21. How much is an airmail stamp? _____ ¢

22. How much is a postcard? _____ ¢

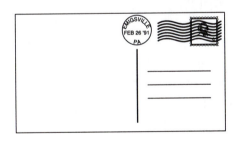

23. How much is an airletter? _____ ¢

16. Read.

B   A

A: I'm going to the supermarket.
B: Why?
A: I need milk.

Copy.

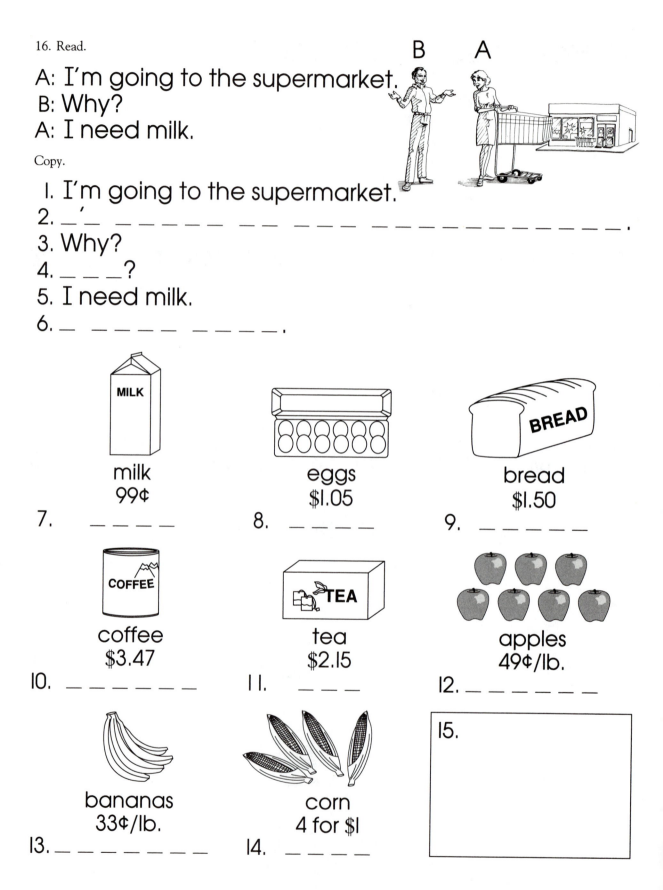

1. I'm going to the supermarket.
2. _ _' _ _ _ _ _ _ _ _   _ _ _ _ _ _ _ _ _ _ _ _ _ _ _.
3. Why?
4. _ _ _ _?
5. I need milk.
6. _ _ _ _ _ _ _ _ _ _ _ _ _.

milk
99¢
7. _ _ _ _ _

eggs
$1.05
8. _ _ _ _ _

bread
$1.50
9. _ _ _ _ _ _

coffee
$3.47
10. _ _ _ _ _ _ _

tea
$2.15
11. _ _ _ _

apples
49¢/lb.
12. _ _ _ _ _ _ _

bananas
33¢/lb.
13. _ _ _ _ _ _ _ _

corn
4 for $1
14. _ _ _ _ _

15.

16. How much is coffee? $ _____

17. How much is bread?   _____

18. How much is milk?   _____

19. How much is tea?   _____

20. How much are eggs?   _____

21. How much are bananas?   _____

22. How much are apples?   _____

23. How much is corn?   _____

17. Go to your supermarket and find out the prices.

1. milk   _____

2. eggs   _____

3. bread   _____

4. coffee   _____

5. tea   _____

6. red apples   _____

7. bananas   _____

8. corn   _____

9. _____   _____

10. _____   _____

18. Read.

A: How much is this balloon?
B: 3¢.
A: I have 5¢.
B: Here. Your change is 2¢.

Draw your change and write how much.

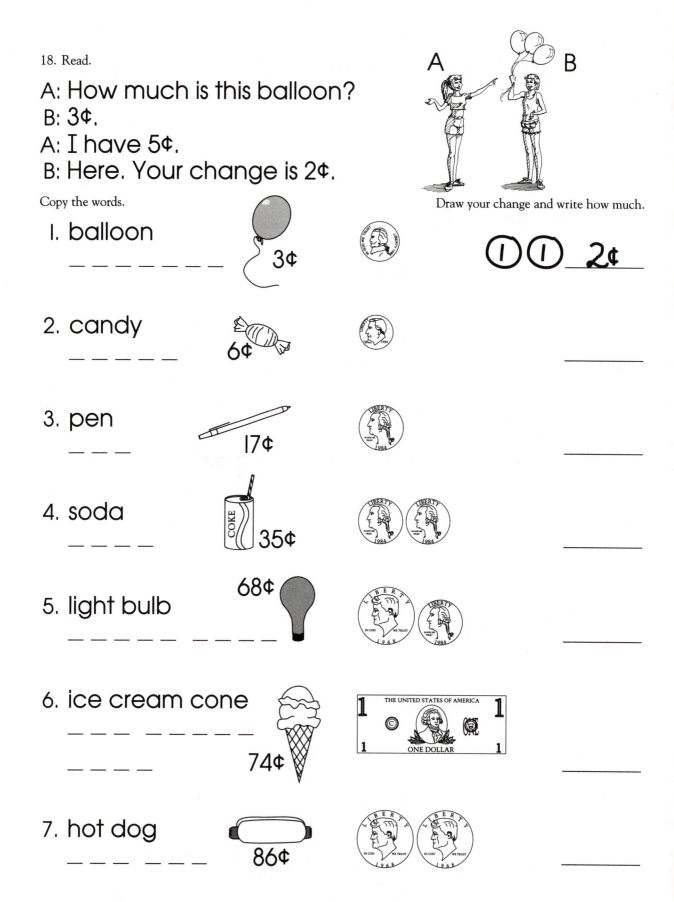

Copy the words.

1. balloon

_ _ _ _ _ _ _

3¢

① ① 2¢

2. candy

_ _ _ _ _

6¢

3. pen

_ _ _

17¢

4. soda

_ _ _ _

35¢

5. light bulb

68¢

_ _ _ _ _ _ _ _ _

6. ice cream cone

_ _ _ _ _ _ _ _

_ _ _ _

74¢

7. hot dog

_ _ _ _ _ _ _

86¢

A: How much is this pineapple?
B: $1.89.
A: I have $2.
B: Here. Your change is _____ ¢.

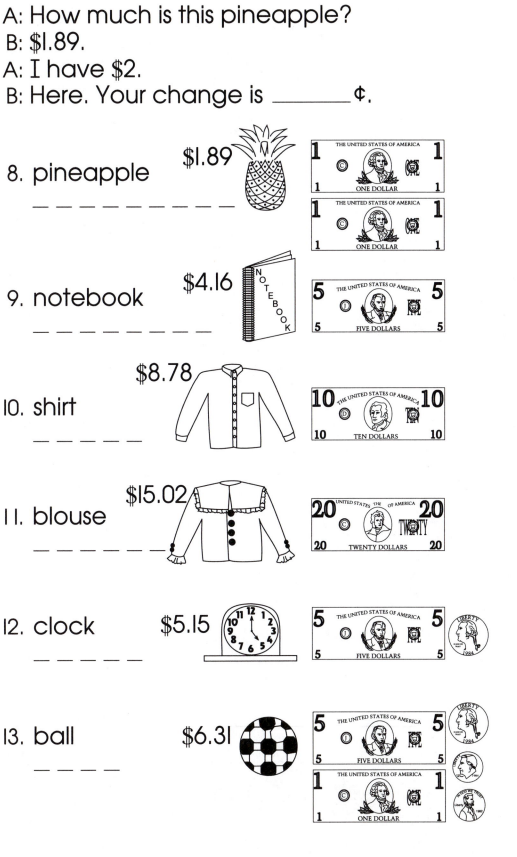

8. pineapple $1.89

_ _ _ _ _ _ _ _ _   _____

9. notebook $4.16

_ _ _ _ _ _ _ _   _____

10. shirt $8.78

_ _ _ _ _   _____

11. blouse $15.02

_ _ _ _ _ _ _   _____

12. clock $5.15

_ _ _ _ _   _____

13. ball $6.31

_ _ _ _ _   _____

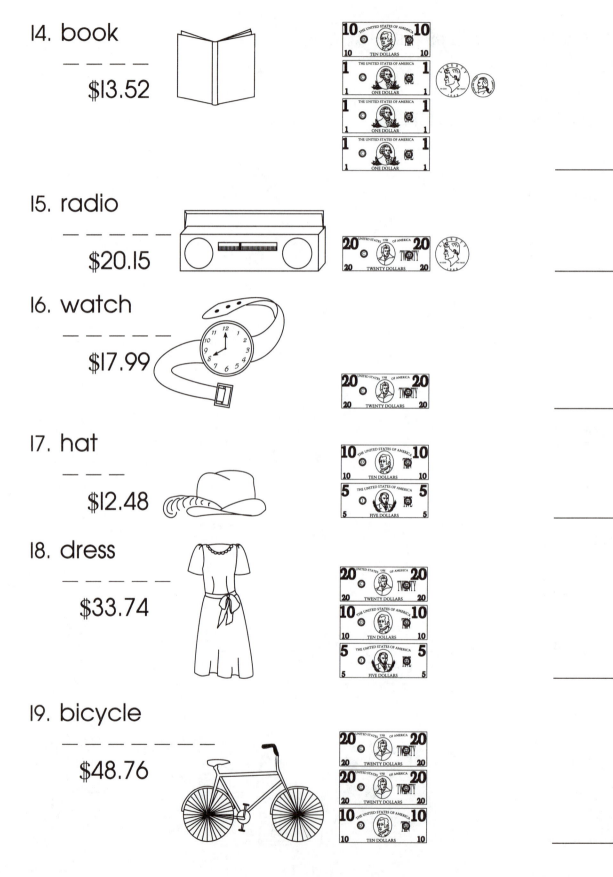

14. book

– – – – –

$13.52

15. radio

– – – – –

$20.15

16. watch

– – – – –

$17.99

17. hat

– – –

$12.48

18. dress

– – – – –

$33.74

19. bicycle

– – – – – –

$48.76

19. Read and copy.

at

1. at _____

2. fat _____

3. cat _____

4. that _____

5. hat _____

at	at	fat	cat	that	hat

20. Read and copy the words.

ou

1. out _____

2. hours _____

3. house _____

My **house** is on Pine Street.

PINE STREET

325

4. blouse _____

I have a white **blouse**.

| ou |
| out   hours   house   blouse |

21. Read and copy the words.

ow

1. now

2. brown

3. down

4. flowers

5. How _____

| ow | now | brown | down | flowers | How |

Who are you angry with?

re you happy?

Sue is scared of mice and snakes.

angry

Dan is very tired.

am sad.

CHAPTER 4

▲▲▲▲▲▲▲▲▲

Feelings

tired

Is he cold?

scared

'm hot and
n very thirsty.

I'm very angry!

hot

cold

homesick

She is very hot.

thirsty

I'm hungry.
I want a hamburger.

Mike is homesick.

Are you hungry?

Sally is scared of spiders.

1. Read and copy.

happy ☺	sad ☹	Yes, I am.	No, I'm not.
_ _ _ _ _	_ _ _	_ _ _ , _ _ _ .	_ _ , _ _ _ _ _ _ .

1. A: Are you **happy**?

   B: Yes, I am. I'm happy.

2. A: Are you **sad**?

   B: Yes, I am. I'm sad.

3. A: Are you **happy**?

   B: No, I'm not. I'm not **happy**.

A B

I am
I'm

A B

2. Write the words.

1. A_ _ y_ _ h_ _ _ _ ?

2. Yes, _ _ _ .

3. I _ _ happy.

4. A_ _ y_ _ s_ _ ?

5. Yes, _ _ _ .

6. I _ _ sad.

7. _re _ou _ad?

8. No, _'_ n_ _ .

9. I'_ _ _ _ sad.

Make a check ☑, and write the words.

10. Are you happy?

11. ☐ Yes, I _ _ .

12. ☐ No, _'_ _ _ _ .

13. ☐ I _ _ h_ _ _ _ .

14. ☐ I'_ not h_ _ _ _ .

15. Are you sad?

16. ☐ Yes, _ _ _ .

17. ☐ No, _'_ _ _ _ .

18. ☐ I _ _ sad.

19. ☐ I _ _ n_ _ s_ _ .

3. Read.

1.

A: I'm **happy** today.
B: Why?
A: Today is my birthday.
B: Oh, happy birthday.
A: Thank you.

2.

A: I'm **sad** today.
B: Why?
A: I'm sick.
B: Oh, I'm sorry.

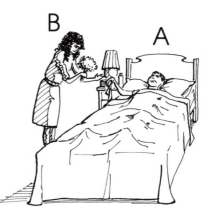

4. Copy the words.

c candles	b balloons	s sad
_ _ _ _ _ _ _	_ _ _ _ _ _ _ _	_ _ _
cake		sick
_ _ _ _		_ _ _ _
candy	birthday	sorry
_ _ _ _ _	_ _ _ _ _ _ _ _	_ _ _ _ _

5. Read and copy.

Yes, **she** is.
___, ___ __.
Yes, **he** is.
___, __ __.

No, **she** isn't.
__, ___ ___.
No, **he** isn't.
__, __ ___.

A: I'm happy.

1.

B: Is she happy?
C: Yes, she is.
    She's happy.

He is
He's
She is
She's

A: I'm sad.

2.

B: Is he sad?
C: Yes, he is. **He's** sad.
B: Is he happy?
C: No, he **isn't**. He **isn't** happy.

is not
isn't

6. Look at the pictures, and write the words.

1. Is s＿＿ happy?

2. Yes, s＿＿ i＿.

3. She ＿＿ happy.

4. Is h＿ sad?

5. No, ＿e i＿＿'t.

6. He ＿＿n't sad.

Make a check ☑, and write the words.

7. Is she happy?

8. ☐ Yes, ＿＿＿ ＿＿.

9. ☐ No, ＿＿＿ ＿＿＿'＿.

10. ☐ She ＿＿ happy.

11. ☐ She ＿＿＿'＿ happy.

12. Is he sad?

13. ☐ Yes, ＿＿ ＿＿.

14. ☐ No, ＿＿ ＿＿＿'＿.

15. ☐ He ＿＿ s＿＿.

16. ☐ He ＿＿＿'＿ sad.

7. Read.

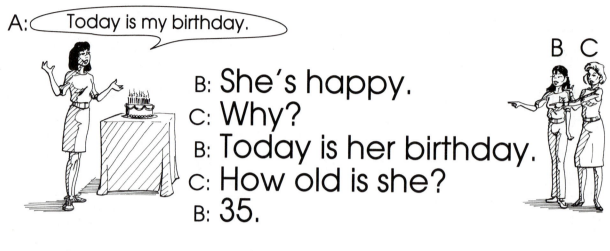

A: Today is my birthday.

B: She's happy.
C: Why?
B: Today is her birthday.
C: How old is she?
B: 35.

1. She's _____.
2. Today is _____ birthday.
3. She's _____ years old.

A: I'm sick.

B: He's sad today.
C: Why?
B: He's sick.
C: Oh, I'm sorry.

4. He's _____ and he's _____.
5. He isn't _____.

8. Read and copy.

Are you . . . ?	Is he . . . ?	Is she . . . ?
___ ___	__ __	__ ___

1. A: Are you **hot**?
   B: Yes, I am. I'm **hot**.
      She's **hot**.
   C:

2. A: Are you **cold**?
   B: Yes, I am. I'm **cold**.
      He's **cold**.
   C:

9. Write the words and make a check ✓.

1. Is she hot?
2. Yes, ___ is.
3. S__ 's h__.

4. Is he cold?
5. Yes, __ is.
6. H_'s c___.

7. Are you hot?
8. ☐ Yes, I __.
9. ☐ No, I'm ___.

10. Are you cold?
11. ☐ Yes, _ am.
12. ☐ No, _'_ not.

13. Is she cold?
14. __, she isn't.

15. Is he hot?
16. __, he isn't.

17. Is she hot?
18. ___, she is.

19. Is he cold?
20. ___, he is.

21. Is she cold?
22. No, ___ isn't.

23. Is he hot?
24. No, he ___'_.

10. Read and copy.

Take off	Put on
_ _ _ _ _ _	_ _ _ _ _ _

jacket _ _ _ _ _ _ _

sweater _ _ _ _ _ _ _

coat _ _ _ _

vest _ _ _ _

11. Read.

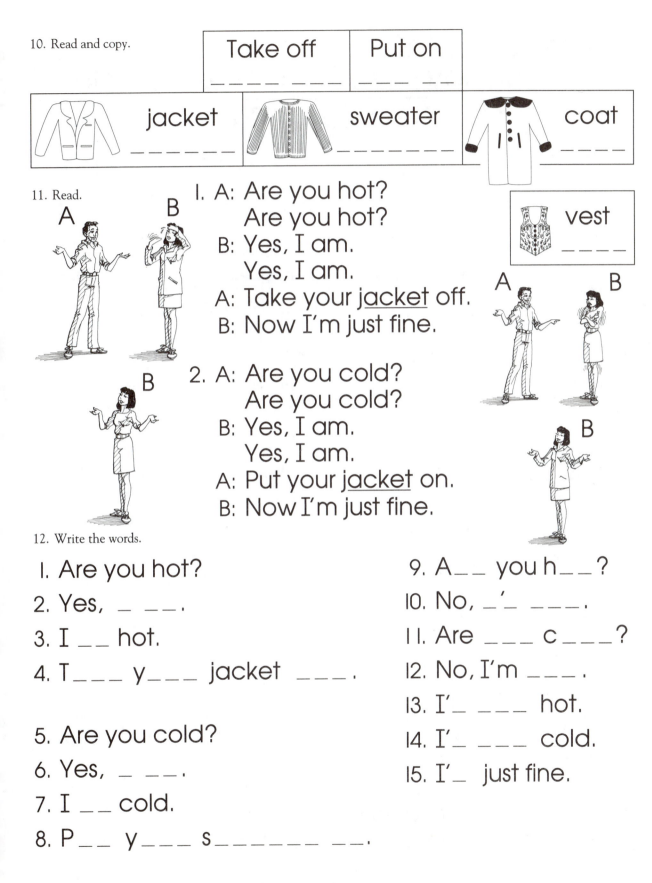

A B

1. A: Are you hot?
   Are you hot?
   B: Yes, I am.
   Yes, I am.
   A: Take your <u>jacket</u> off.
   B: Now I'm just fine.

2. A: Are you cold?
   Are you cold?
   B: Yes, I am.
   Yes, I am.
   A: Put your <u>jacket</u> on.
   B: Now I'm just fine.

12. Write the words.

1. Are you hot?

2. Yes, _ _ _.

3. I _ _ hot.

4. T_ _ _ y_ _ _ jacket _ _ _.

5. Are you cold?

6. Yes, _ _ _.

7. I _ _ cold.

8. P_ _ y_ _ _ s_ _ _ _ _ _ _ _ _.

9. A_ _ you h_ _?

10. No, _'_ _ _ _.

11. Are _ _ _ c_ _ _?

12. No, I'm _ _ _.

13. I'_ _ _ _ hot.

14. I'_ _ _ _ cold.

15. I'_ just fine.

13. Read and use these words in the sentences below.

I'm He's She's	happy	hot
	sad	cold

Yes	No
I am he is she is	I'm not he isn't she isn't

Write the words.

1. _____ you happy?
2. Yes, I _____.

3. _____ she sad?
4. No, she _____.

5. _____ he hot?
6. Yes, _____ is.

7. Is _____ cold?
8. No, she _____.

9. Are you sad?
10. _____, _____ _____.

11. He _____ happy.
12. I _____ cold.
13. She _____ sad.
14. I _____ not sad.
15. She _____ not happy.
16. He _____ not cold.

17. He _____ cold.
18. She is _____.
19. I am _____.
20. _____ is sad.
21. Is _____ sad?.
22. _____ 's hot.
23. _____ she hot?
24. _____ isn't hot.
25. _____ ' ___ happy.
26. _____ he happy?
27. Yes, he _____.
28. No, he _____.
29. _____, he isn't.
30. _____, I am.
31. _____, she is.
32. Are _____ hot?
33. Is _____ cold?
34. _____ he happy?
35. Yes, _____ is.
36. No, _____ isn't.
37. Yes, _____ am.
38. No, _____ not.

14. Read and copy.

very	hungry	thirsty
_ _ _ _	_ _ _ _ _ _	_ _ _ _ _ _ _

1. A: Are you **hungry**?
   B: Yes, I am. I'm very **hungry**.

He's **hungry**.

2. A: Are you **hungry**?
   B: No, I'm not. I'm not **hungry**. I'm very **thirsty**.

She isn't **hungry**. She's **thirsty**.

15. Make a check ✔, and write the words.

1. Is **he** hungry?
☐ 2. Yes, _ _ _ _ .
☐ 3. No, _ _ _ _ _ ' _ .

4. Is **she** thirsty?
☐ 5. Yes, _ _ _ _ _ .
☐ 6. No, _ _ _ _ _ _ ' _ .

7. Are you hungry?
☐ 8. Yes, I _ _ .
9. I _ _ very h _ _ _ _ _ .
☐ 10. No, I'm _ _ _ .
11. I'm _ _ _ hungry.

12. Are you thirsty?
☐ 13. Yes, _ _ _ .
14. I _ _ v _ _ _ th _ _ _ _ _ .
☐ 15. No, _ ' _ _ _ _ .
16. I' _ _ _ _ thirsty.

71

16. Read.

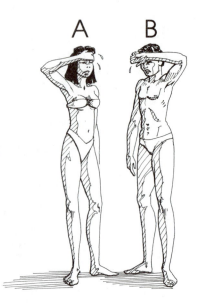

A B

1.
  A: It's hot today.
  B: Yes, it's very hot today.

2.
  A: I'm hot and very thirsty.
  B: Me, too.

3.
  A: I want some coffee.
  B: I want a Coke.

Copy and write other drinks.

1. I want **some** coffee.

   _ ____ ____ _____.

2. I want **some** tea.

   _ ____ ____ _____.

3. I want **some** water.

   _ ____ ____ _____.

4. I want **some** _____.

5. I want **a** Coke.

   _ ____ _ _____.

6. I want **a** 7-up.

   _ ____ _ _____.

7. I want **a** _____.

17. Read.

1. A: I'm hungry.
   B: Me, too.

2. A: I want some chicken.
   B: I want a sandwich.

Copy and write other foods.

1. I want **some** chicken.
   _ ____ ____ _____.

2. I want **some** fish.
   _ ____ ____ _____.

3. I want **some** rice.
   _ ____ ____ _____.

4. I want **some** beans.
   _ ____ ____ _____.

5. I want **some** _____.

6. I want **a** sandwich.
   _ ____ _ _____.

7. I want **a** hot dog.
   _ ____ _ _____.

8. I want **a** hamburger.
   _ ____ _ _____.

9. I want **a** banana.
   _ ____ _ _____.

10. I want **an** apple.
    _ ____ __ _____.

11. I want **a** _____.

18. Read and copy.

homesick	think about	country
_ _ _ _ _ _ _ _	_ _ _ _ _ _ _ _ _ _	_ _ _ _ _ _ _

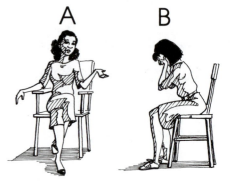

1. A: Are you **homesick**?
   B: Yes, I am. I'm **homesick**.
   I think about my country,
   and I'm sad.

2. A: Are you **homesick**?
   B: No, I'm not. I'm not **homesick**.
   I'm happy here.

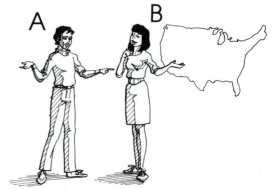

19. Write the words and make a check ☑.

1. Are you homesick?
   ☐ 2. Yes, _ _ _ .
   3. I'_ h_ _ _ _ _ _ _ _ .
   4. I th_ _ _ about my country, and I'_ s_ _ .

   ☐ 5. No, I'm _ _ _ .
   6. I'_ _ _ _ h_ _ _ _ _ _ _ .
   7. I'm h_ _ _ _ h_ _ _ .

8. What country are you f_ _ _?
9. I'm from _____ .

20. Read and copy.

very	angry	tired
_ _ _ _	_ _ _ _ _	_ _ _ _ _
scared	homesick	thirsty
_ _ _ _ _ _	_ _ _ _ _ _ _ _	_ _ _ _ _ _ _

We are
We're

I. A: Are you **scared**?
   B: Yes, I am. I'm very **scared**.

2. A: Are you **angry**?
   B: Yes, I am. I'm very **angry**.
   A: Me, too.

We're very **angry**.

21. Write the words and make a check ✔.

☐ I. I _ _ scared.
☐ 2. I'_ not scared.

   3. Are you hungry?
☐ 4. Yes, _ _ _ .
☐ 5. No, _'_ _ _ _ .

   6. She _ _ very thirsty.
   7. _ _ _ isn't thirsty.

   8. Is he angry?
   9. Yes, _ _ _ _ .
   10. No, _ _ _ _ _'_ .

11. Is she homesick?
12. Yes, _ _ _ is.
13. She _ _ very homesick.

We're **tired**.

14. Are you tired?
☐ 15. Yes, _ _ _ .
    16. I _ _ very t _ _ _ _ .
☐ 17. No, _'_ _ _ _ .
    18. I'm _ _ _ t _ _ _ _ .

22. Read and copy the words.

scared of	angry with
_ _ _ _ _ _ _ _	_ _ _ _ _ _ _ _ _

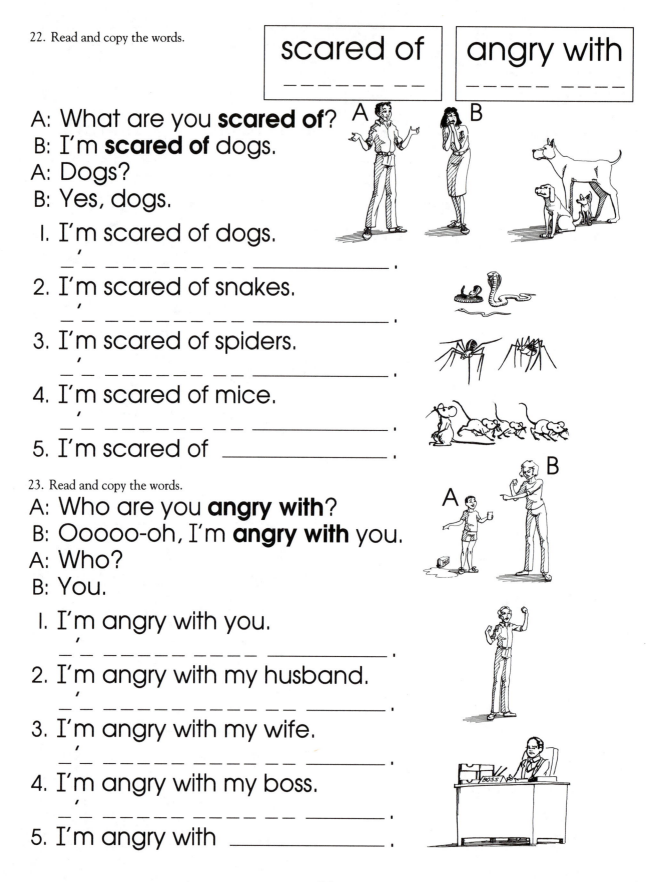

A: What are you **scared of**? A   B

B: I'm **scared of** dogs.

A: Dogs?

B: Yes, dogs.

1. I'm scared of dogs.

_ _ _ _ _ _ _ _ _ _ _ _ _ .

2. I'm scared of snakes.

_ _ _ _ _ _ _ _ _ _ _ _ _ .

3. I'm scared of spiders.

_ _ _ _ _ _ _ _ _ _ _ _ _ .

4. I'm scared of mice.

_ _ _ _ _ _ _ _ _ _ _ _ _ .

5. I'm scared of _ _ _ _ _ _ _ .

23. Read and copy the words.

A: Who are you **angry with**?

B: Ooooo-oh, I'm **angry with** you.

A: Who?

B: You.

1. I'm angry with you.

_ _ _ _ _ _ _ _ _ _ _ _ _ _ .

2. I'm angry with my husband.

_ _ _ _ _ _ _ _ _ _ _ _ _ _ .

3. I'm angry with my wife.

_ _ _ _ _ _ _ _ _ _ _ _ _ _ .

4. I'm angry with my boss.

_ _ _ _ _ _ _ _ _ _ _ _ _ _ .

5. I'm angry with _ _ _ _ _ _ _ .

24. Read and copy.

are

_ _ _ _

are not

_ _ _ _ _ _

aren't

_ _ _ _ _

Yes, they are.

_ _ _, _ _ _ _ _ _ _.

No, they aren't.

_ _, _ _ _ _ _ _ _ _ _ _.

Read the questions, make a check ✔, and write the words.

They are happy.

1.

2. Are they happy?
   ☐ Yes, they are.
   ☐ No, they aren't.

They are angry.

3.

4. Are they hungry?
   ☐ Yes, they _ _ _.
   ☐ No, they _ _ _ _'_.

They are sad.

5.

6. Are they sick?
   ☐ Yes, _ _ _ _ are.
   ☐ No, _ _ _ _ aren't.

They are thirsty.

7.

8. Are they tired?
   ☐ Yes, _ _ _ _ _ _ _ .
   ☐ No, _ _ _ _ _ _ _ _'_.

25. Read and copy the words.

We	He	She	Please	me	tea	Be	See
——	——	———	——————	——	———	——	———

1.
2.   My husband and I are very happy.
     We   are very happy.

   We --

3.
4.   My wife and I are very happy.
     We   are very happy.

   We --

5. **He** is very scared.

   He --

6.
She is very tired.

She _____

7.
Please, give **me** some **tea.**

Please _____

me _____

tea _____

8. **Be** careful.

Be _____

9.
See you tomorrow.

See _____

| We | He | She | Please | me | tea | Be | See |

26. Read and copy the words.

B b

1. ball

How much is the **ball**?

It's $9.99.

2. balloon

I have a red **balloon**.

3. bus

The **bus** is late.

4. bicycle

I want a **bicycle** for my **birthday**.

5. birthday

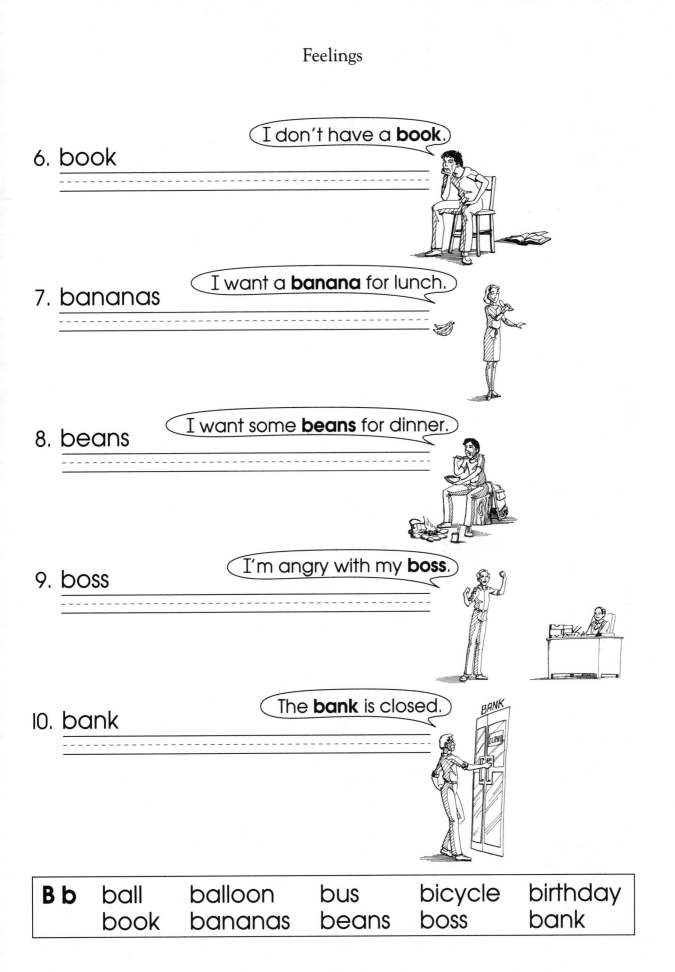

6. book

7. bananas

8. beans

9. boss

10. bank

| **B b** | ball | balloon | bus | bicycle | birthday |
| | book | bananas | beans | boss | bank |

27. Read and copy the words.

H h

1. hot

2. hot dog

3. his

4. hat

5. her

6. happy

7. He

8. hungry

9. hamburger

10. homesick

It's **hot** today.

The **hot dog** is $2.00.

His hat is brown.

Her hat is red.

I'm **happy** today.

He's very **hungry**.

I'm **hungry**. I want a **hamburger**.

She's very **homesick**.

11. husband

This is my **husband**.

Hi.

12. Hi

13. hospital

My friend is in the **hospital**.

HOSPITAL

14. house

My **house** is on Pine Street.

410

PINE STREET

15. home

Bye. I'm going **home**.

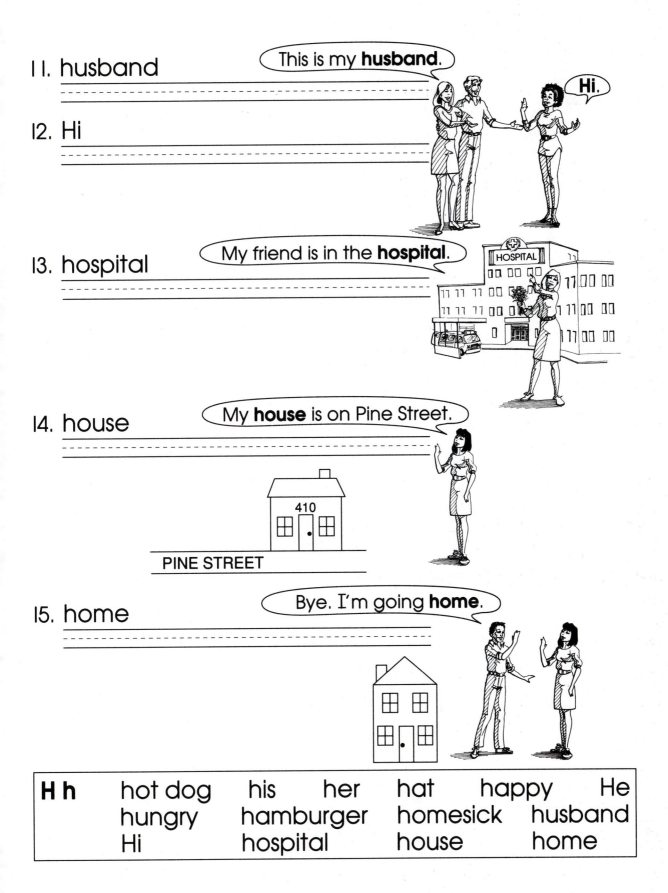

H h	hot dog	his	her	hat	happy	He
	hungry	hamburger		homesick	husband	
	Hi	hospital		house	home	

e you divorced?

How many children do you have?

This is my father and mother.

daughter

ingle

They have one child.

x-husband

widowed

My wife died.
m widowed.

married

CHAPTER 5

▲▲▲▲▲▲▲▲▲▲

Family

wife

ivorced

Mrs.

I am single.

son

Mr.

this your sister?

parents

I have one daughter and one son.

father

This is my wife.

This is my brother.

I am married.
have two children.

Miss

1. Read and copy the words.

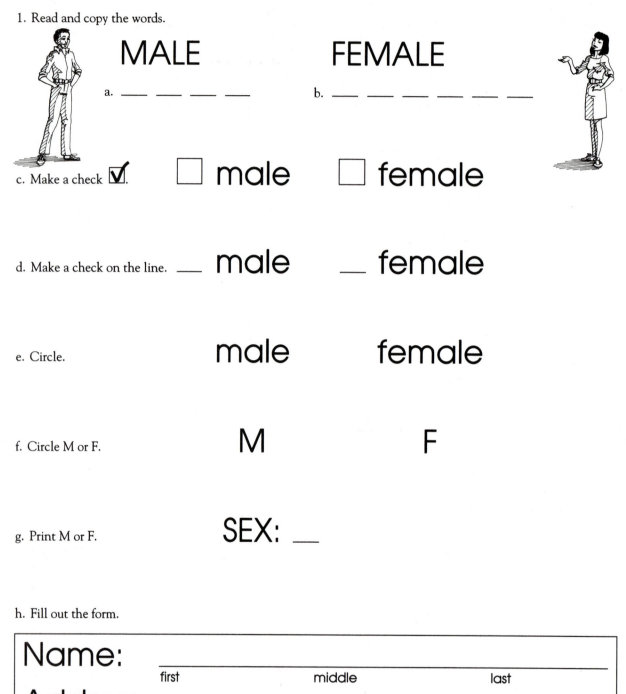

MALE   FEMALE

a. __ __ __ __   b. __ __ __ __ __ __

c. Make a check ✓. ☐ male   ☐ female

d. Make a check on the line. __ male   __ female

e. Circle. male   female

f. Circle M or F. M   F

g. Print M or F. SEX: __

h. Fill out the form.

Name:	_____		
	first	middle	last
Address:	_____		
	number street		apt. #
	_____		
	city	state	zip code
Sex:	☐ male	☐ female	

Family

2. Read and copy the words.

married	single	widowed	divorced
1. _ _ _ _ _ _ _ _	2. _ _ _ _ _ _ _	3. _ _ _ _ _ _ _ _	4. _ _ _ _ _ _ _ _

We're married.
5. _ _ ' _ _   _ _ _ _ _ _ _ _ .

I'm single.
6. _ ' _   _ _ _ _ _ _ _ .

I'm single.
7. _ ' _   _ _ _ _ _ _ .

My husband died.
8. _ _   _ _ _ _ _ _ _ _   _ _ _ _ .

I'm widowed.
9. _ ' _   _ _ _ _ _ _ _ .

My wife died.
10. _ _   _ _ _ _   _ _ _ _ .

I'm widowed.
11. _ ' _   _ _ _ _ _ _ _ .

Bye-bye. I don't love you.
12. _ _ _ _ - _ _ _ . _ _ _ _ ' _   _ _ _ _   _ _ _ .

I'm divorced.
13. _ ' _   _ _ _ _ _ _ _ _ .

Bye-bye.
14. _ _ _ _ - _ _ _ .

I'm divorced.
15. _ ' _   _ _ _ _ _ _ _ _ .

Make a check ☑.

16. Are you married?   ☐ Yes   ☐ No
17. Are you single?   ☐ Yes   ☐ No
18. Are you widowed?   ☐ Yes   ☐ No
19. Are you divorced?   ☐ Yes   ☐ No

3. Write the words and make a check 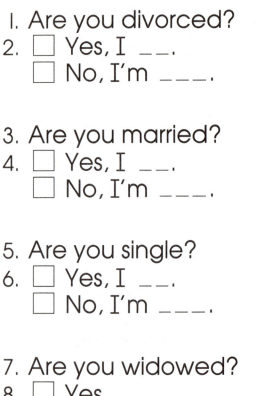.

1. Are you divorced?
2. ☐ Yes, I __.
   ☐ No, I'm ___.

3. Are you married?
4. ☐ Yes, I __.
   ☐ No, I'm ___.

5. Are you single?
6. ☐ Yes, I __.
   ☐ No, I'm ___.

7. Are you widowed?
8. ☐ Yes, _ __.
   ☐ No, _'_ ___.

Fill out the form. Please print.

9.

Name:	_____	_____	_____
	first	middle	last
Address:	_____		_____
	number street		apt. #
	_____	_____	_____
	city	state	zip code

☐ male   ☐ married
☐ female   ☐ single
               ☐ widowed
               ☐ divorced

4. Read and copy the words.

married	single
_ _ _ _ _ _ _	_ _ _ _ _ _

husband	wife	boyfriend	girlfriend
_ _ _ _ _ _ _	_ _ _ _	_ _ _ _ _ _ _ _ _	_ _ _ _ _ _ _ _ _ _

1. A: Are you married?
   B: Yes, I am. This is my husband.
   A: Oh.

2. A: Are you married?
   B: Yes, I am. This is my wife.
   A: Oh.

3. A: Are you married?
   B: No, I'm not. I'm single.
      This is my boyfriend.
   A: Oh.

4. A: Are you married?
   B: No, I'm not. I'm single.
      This is my girlfriend.
   A: Oh.

5. Read and copy the words.

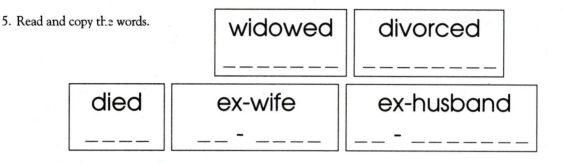

widowed	divorced
_ _ _ _ _ _ _	_ _ _ _ _ _ _

died	ex-wife	ex-husband
_ _ _ _	_ _ - _ _ _ _	_ _ - _ _ _ _ _ _ _

I. A: Are you married?
   B: No, I'm not. My wife died.
      I'm widowed.
   A: Oh, I'm sorry.
   B: That's OK.

2. A: Are you married?
   B: No, I'm not. My husband died.
      I'm widowed.
   A: Oh, I'm sorry.
   B: That's OK.

3. A: Are you married?
   B: No, I'm not. I'm divorced.
      My ex-wife is in Hong Kong.
   A: Oh.

4. A: Are you married?
   B: No, I'm not. I'm divorced.
      My ex-husband is in Los Angeles.
   A: Oh.

6.

a. Read and copy the words.

Mr.	Mrs.	Miss
___	_____	_____

A   B

married	single	widowed
_____	_____	_____

b. Read.

A: How do you do? My name is **Mr.** Kay.

B: Hi. My name is **Miss** Lee.

c. Read, check <u>one</u> ☑, and write your last name.

☐ I am married. My name is **Mrs.** _____.
  last name

☐ I am married. My name is **Mr.** _____.
  last name

☐ I am single. My name is **Miss** _____.
  last name

☐ I am single. My name is **Mr.** _____.
  last name

☐ I am widowed. My husband died.
  My name is **Mrs.** _____.
  last name

☐ I am widowed. My wife died.
  My name is **Mr.** _____.
  last name

d. Circle (Miss, Mrs., or Mr.) Then print your name.

Miss

Mrs.

Mr. _____, _____ _____
        last   first   middle

e. Make a check ☑. Then print your name.

☐ Miss
☐ Mrs.
☐ Mr. _____
        first   middle   last

7.

married
1. _ _ _ _ _ _ _

Read.

2. They are married.
3. He is the husband.
4. She is the wife.
5. They are husband and wife.

Write the words and make a check ☑.

6. He is the _ _ _ _ _ _ _.
7. She is the _ _ _ _.
8. They are m _ _ _ _ _ _.
9. _ _ _ _ _ _ _ husband _ _ _ wife.
10. Is he married?
    ☐ 11. Yes, he _ _.
    ☐ 12. No, he _ _ _ ' _.
13. He _ _ married.
14. Is she married?
    ☐ 15. Yes, she _ _.
    ☐ 16. No, she _ _ _ ' _.
17. She is m _ _ _ _ _ _.

single
18. _ _ _ _ _ _

19. He is single.
20. He is not married.

21. He's _ _ _ _ _ _.
22. He isn't _ _ _ _ _ _ _.
23. Is he single?
    ☐ 24. Yes, he _ _.
    ☐ 25. No, he _ _ _ ' _.
26. Is he married?
    ☐ 27. Yes, he _ _.
    ☐ 28. No, he _ _ _ ' _.

29. She is single.
30. She is not married.

31. She's _ _ _ _ _ _ _.
32. She isn't _ _ _ _ _ _ _.
33. Is she single?
    ☐ 34. Yes, she _ _.
    ☐ 35. No, she _ _ _ ' _.
36. Is she married?
    ☐ 37. Yes, she _ _.
    ☐ 38. No, she _ _ _ ' _.

8. Copy.

one pen

1. ___ ___

one pencil

3. ___ ___

two pens

2. ___ ___ ___

two pencils

4. ___ ___ ___

Read.

5. A: Do you have a pen?
   B: No, I don't.

   A: Do you have a pencil?
   B: Yes, I do.

   A: How many pencils do you have?
   B: I have two pencils.

A   B

9. Answer the questions. Make a check ☑.

1. Do you have a pen?
2. ☐ Yes, I do.
   ☐ No, I don't.

3. Do you have a pencil?
4. ☐ Yes, I do.
   ☐ No, I don't.

5. ☐ I h___ a pen.
6. ☐ I don't h___
      a pen.

7. ☐ I h___ a pencil.
8. ☐ I don't h___
      a pencil.

9. How many pens do
   you have?
10. ☐ I have one pen.
    ☐ I have _____ pens.
              #
    ☐ I don't have a pen.

11. How many pencils do
    you have?
12. ☐ I have one pencil.
    ☐ I have _____ pencils.
              #
    ☐ I don't have a pencil.

10. Read, copy, make a check 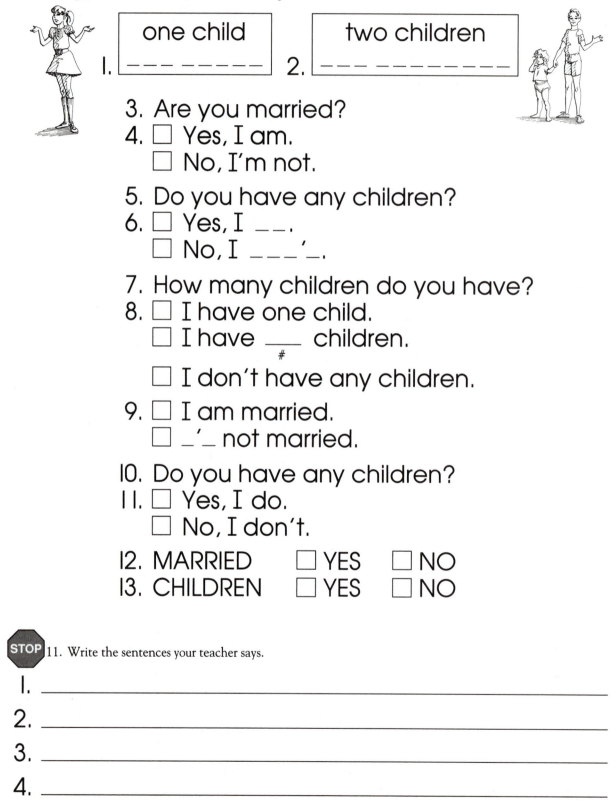, and answer the questions.

one child	two children
1. _ _ _ _ _ _ _	2. _ _ _ _ _ _ _ _ _ _

3. Are you married?
4. ☐ Yes, I am.
   ☐ No, I'm not.

5. Do you have any children?
6. ☐ Yes, I _ _.
   ☐ No, I _ _ _ ' _.

7. How many children do you have?
8. ☐ I have one child.
   ☐ I have _ _ _ children.

#
   ☐ I don't have any children.

9. ☐ I am married.
   ☐ _ ' _ not married.

10. Do you have any children?
11. ☐ Yes, I do.
    ☐ No, I don't.

12. MARRIED   ☐ YES   ☐ NO
13. CHILDREN   ☐ YES   ☐ NO

STOP 11. Write the sentences your teacher says.

1. _____

2. _____

3. _____

4. _____

12. Read and copy.

I am	I do	I don't	I have
_ __	_ __	_ ____	_ ____
We are	We do	We don't	We have
__ ___	__ __	__ ____	__ ____

1. A: Are you married?
   B: No, I'm not. I'm single.

2. A: Are you married?
   B: Yes, I am.
   A: Do you have any children?
   B: Yes, I do.
   A: How many children do you have?
   B: I have two children.

3. A: Are you married?
   B: Yes, we are.
   A: Do you have any children?
   B: No, we don't. We don't have any children.

4. A: Are you married?
   B: Yes, we are.
   A: Do you have any children?
   B: Yes, we do.
   A: How many children do you have?
   B: We have one child.

5. A: Are you married?
   B: Yes, we are.
   A: Do you have any children?
   B: Yes, we do.
   A: How many children do you have?
   B: We have three children.

13. Read and copy. Look at the pictures. Then say who is what.

a family	mother	father
_ _ _ _ _ _ _ _	_ _ _ _ _ _	_ _ _ _ _ _

son	sons	daughter	daughters
_ _ _	_ _ _ _	_ _ _ _ _ _ _ _	_ _ _ _ _ _ _ _ _ _

1.

2.

3.

4.

5.

6.

7.

8.

14. Make a check ☑, and answer the questions.

1. Do you have any **sons**?
2. ☐ Yes, I do.
   ☐ No, I don't.

3. Do you have any **daughters**?
4. ☐ Yes, I do.
   ☐ No, I don't.

5. How many **sons** do you have?
6. ☐ I have one son.
   ☐ I have __ sons.
        #
   ☐ I don't have any sons.

7. How many **daughters** do you have?
8. ☐ I have one daughter.
   ☐ I have __ daughters.
        #
   ☐ I don't have any daughters.

15. Look at the pictures and answer the questions. Write the ages.

1. How old are your children?

2. I have three daughters.
3. One is ___ ; one is ___ ; and one is ___.
    age   age   age

4. I have two sons.
5. One is ___ , and one is ___.
    age   age

6. I have one son.
7. He is ___ years old.
    age

8. I have one daughter.
9. She is ___ years old.
    age

10. I have two daughters.
11. One is ___ , and one is ___.
    age   age

12. I have four sons.
13. One is ___ ; one is ___ ; one is ___ ; and one is ___.
    age   age   age   age

14. I have twins.
15. They are ___ years old.
    age

16. Write the words.

1. One __ 30 years old,   4. She __ 20 years old.
2. and o___ is 28.   5. They ___ 10 years old.
3. He __ 15 years old.   6. I __ ___ years old.
                                    age

98

17. Write the words and make a check ☑. Stand up and tell the class about your family.

My Family

I. _ _   _ _ _ _ _ _

2. My name is _____ .
   first   (middle)   last

3. I am from _____ .
                      country

4. I speak _____ .
                   language/s

5. My birthdate is _____ .
                birthdate (month-day-year)

6. I am _____ .
   ☐ married   ☐ single   ☐ widowed   ☐ divorced

7. ☐ I have one child.
   ☐ I have ___ children.
            #
   ☐ I don't have any children.

8. ☐ I have one son. He is ___.
                          age
   ☐ I have ___ sons.
            #
   They are ___, ___, ___, ___, ___, and ___.
            age age age age age   age
   ☐ I don't have any sons.

9. ☐ I have one daughter. She is ___.
                               age
   ☐ I have ___ daughters.
            #
   They are ___, ___, ___, ___, ___, and ___.
            age age age age age   age
   ☐ I don't have any daughters.

18. Read and write the words.

A.

a boy   a girl   a baby

1._ ___   2._ ____   3._ _____

children

4. _____

B.

a man   a woman

5. _ ___   6. _ _____

the husband   the wife

7. ___   8. ___

_____   ____

C.

a mother   a father

10. _ _____   11. _ _____

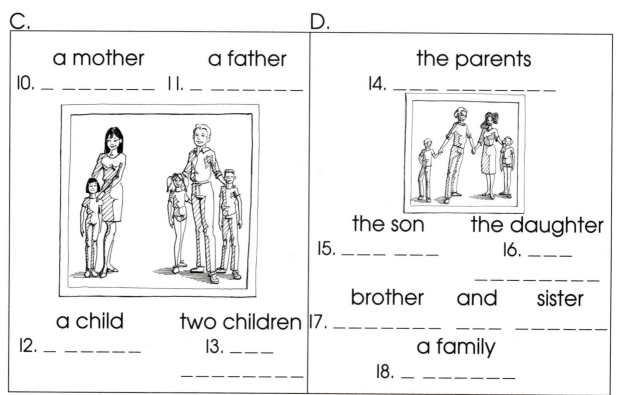

a child   two children

12. _ _____   13. ___

_____

D.

the parents

14. ___ _____

the son   the daughter

15. ___ ___   16. ___

_____

brother   and   sister

17. _____ ___ _____

a family

18. _ _____

19. Write **He**, **She**, or **They**.

Look at picture A.

1. __ is a boy.
2. ___ is a girl.
3. __ is a baby.
4. ____ are children.

Look at picture B.

5. __ is a man.
6. ___ is a woman.
7. __ is the husband.
8. ___ is the wife.
9. ____ are husband and wife.

Look at picture C.

10. ___ is a mother.
11. __ is a father.
12. ____ is a child.
13. ____ are children.

Look at picture D.

14. ____ are the parents.
15. __ is the son.
16. ___ is the daughter.
17. ____ are brother and sister.
18. ____ are a family.

20. Read.

1. A: This is my wife, my son, and my daughter.
   B: Hi. Nice to meet you.

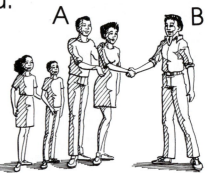

2. A: This is my mother and this is my father.
   B: Hi. Nice to meet you.
   A: This is my sister and this is my baby brother.
   B: Hi. Nice to meet you, too.

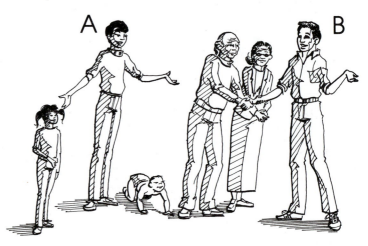

3. A: This is my friend.
   B: Hi.
   C: Nice to meet you.
   B: Nice to meet you, too.

21. Read. Make a check ☑. Answer the questions.

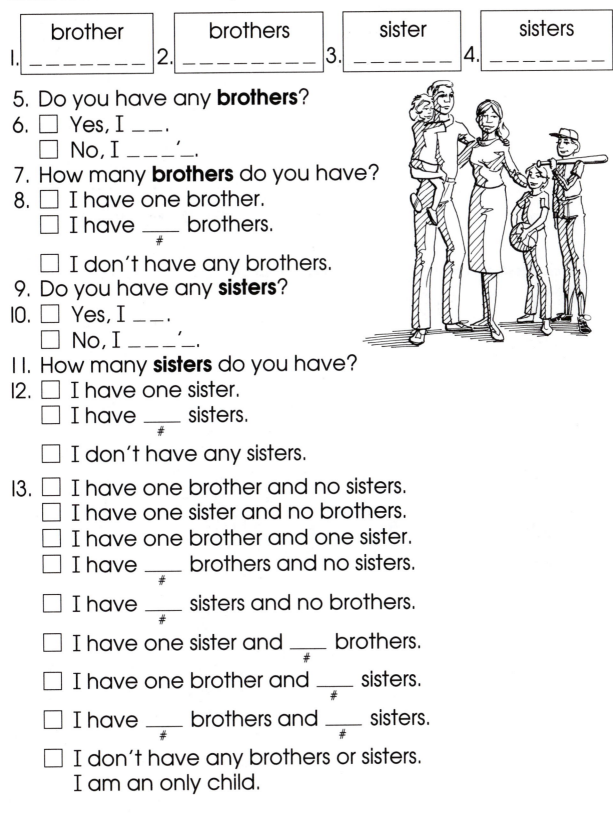

| 1. | brother
_ _ _ _ _ _ _ | 2. | brothers
_ _ _ _ _ _ _ _ _ | 3. | sister
_ _ _ _ _ _ | 4. | sisters
_ _ _ _ _ _ _ |

5. Do you have any **brothers**?
6. ☐ Yes, I _ _.
   ☐ No, I _ _ _ _'_.
7. How many **brothers** do you have?
8. ☐ I have one brother.
   ☐ I have ___ brothers.
   #

   ☐ I don't have any brothers.
9. Do you have any **sisters**?
10. ☐ Yes, I _ _.
    ☐ No, I _ _ _ _'_.
11. How many **sisters** do you have?
12. ☐ I have one sister.
    ☐ I have ___ sisters.
    #

    ☐ I don't have any sisters.

13. ☐ I have one brother and no sisters.
    ☐ I have one sister and no brothers.
    ☐ I have one brother and one sister.
    ☐ I have ___ brothers and no sisters.
    #

    ☐ I have ___ sisters and no brothers.
    #

    ☐ I have one sister and ___ brothers.
    #

    ☐ I have one brother and ___ sisters.
    #

    ☐ I have ___ brothers and ___ sisters.
    #   #

    ☐ I don't have any brothers or sisters.
    I am an only child.

22. Read and write the words.

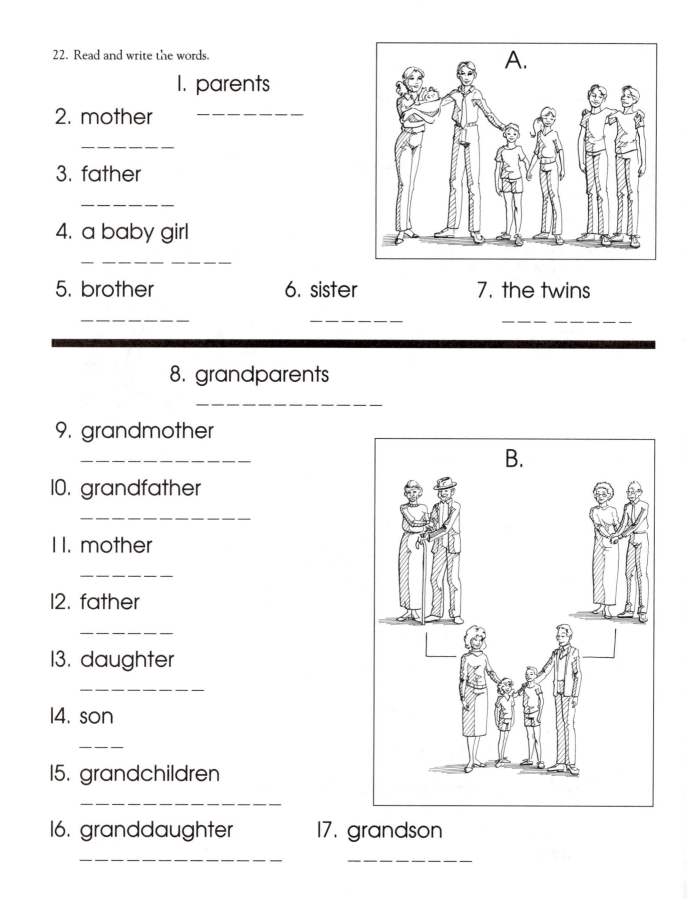

1. parents

2. mother — — — — — — —
— — — — — —

3. father
— — — — — —

4. a baby girl
— — — — — — — —

5. brother
— — — — — — —

6. sister
— — — — — —

7. the twins
— — — — — — —

8. grandparents
— — — — — — — — — — — —

9. grandmother
— — — — — — — — — — —

10. grandfather
— — — — — — — — — — —

11. mother
— — — — — —

12. father
— — — — — —

13. daughter
— — — — — — —

14. son
— — —

15. grandchildren
— — — — — — — — — — —

16. granddaughter
— — — — — — — — — — — —

17. grandson
— — — — — — — —

Family

23. Write **He**, **She**, or **They**.

Look at picture A.

1. _ _ _ _ are the parents.
2. _ _ _ is the mother.
3. _ _ is the father.
4. _ _ _ is a baby girl.
5. _ _ is the brother.
6. _ _ _ is the sister.
7. _ _ _ _ are the twins.

Look at picture B.

8. _ _ _ _ are the grandparents.
9. _ _ _ is a grandmother.
10. _ _ is a grandfather.
11. _ _ _ is the mother.
12. _ _ is the father.
13. _ _ _ is the daughter.
14. _ _ is the son.
15. _ _ _ _ are the grandchildren.
16. _ _ _ is the granddaughter.
17. _ _ is the grandson.

24. Read and copy the words.

mother and father parents	grandmother and grandfather grandparents
_____	_____

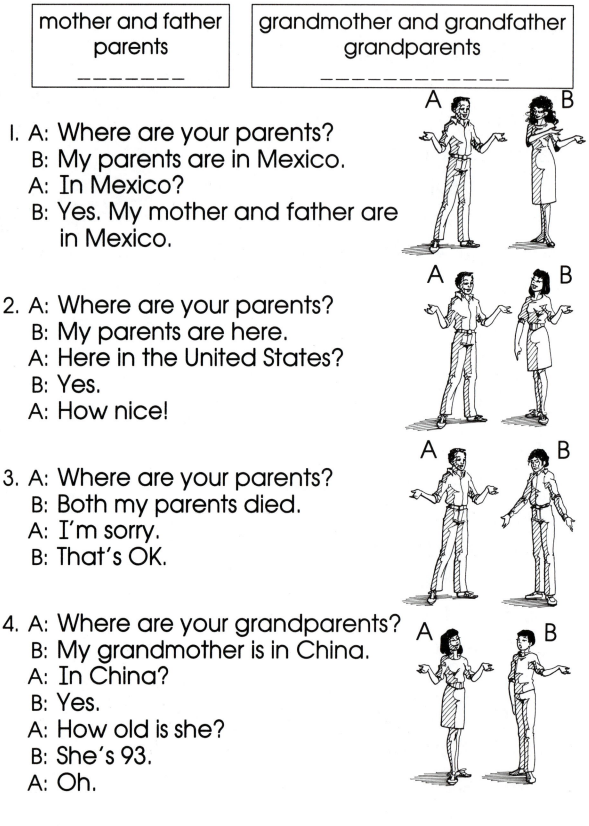

1. A: Where are your parents?
   B: My parents are in Mexico.
   A: In Mexico?
   B: Yes. My mother and father are
      in Mexico.

2. A: Where are your parents?
   B: My parents are here.
   A: Here in the United States?
   B: Yes.
   A: How nice!

3. A: Where are your parents?
   B: Both my parents died.
   A: I'm sorry.
   B: That's OK.

4. A: Where are your grandparents?
   B: My grandmother is in China.
   A: In China?
   B: Yes.
   A: How old is she?
   B: She's 93.
   A: Oh.

25. Read, answer the questions, and make a check ✓.

1. Where are your **parents**?
2. ☐ My mother is in _____.
   ☐ My father is in _____.
   ☐ Both my parents are in _____.
   ☐ My mother died.
   ☐ My father died.
   ☐ Both my parents died.

3. How many **grandparents** do you have?
4. ☐ 0
   ☐ 1
   ☐ 2
   ☐ 3
   ☐ 4

5. How many **grandmothers** do you have?
6. ☐ one grandmother
   ☐ two grandmothers
   ☐ Both died.

7. How many **grandfathers** do you have?
8. ☐ one grandfather
   ☐ two grandfathers
   ☐ Both died.

STOP 26. Write the sentences your teacher says.

1. _____
2. _____
3. _____
4. _____
5. _____

27. Read.

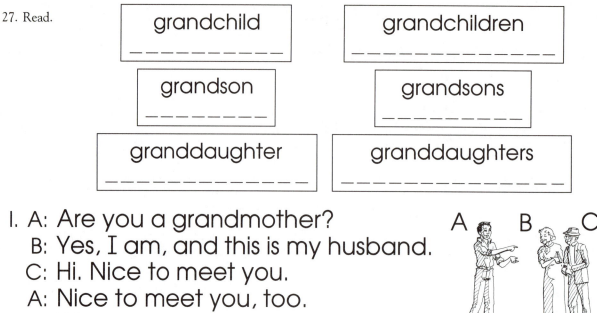

grandchild	grandchildren
_____	_____

grandson	grandsons
_____	_____

granddaughter	granddaughters
_____	_____

1. A: Are you a grandmother?
   B: Yes, I am, and this is my husband.
   C: Hi. Nice to meet you.
   A: Nice to meet you, too.
   C: We are grandparents.

2. A: How many grandchildren do you have?
   B: We have three grandchildren.
   C: Two grandsons and one granddaughter.
   A: How nice!

3. A: How old are your grandchildren?
   B: My granddaughter is 12 and . . .
   C: and one grandson is 10 and one is 8.
   A: Oh.

Family

28. Read and copy.

grandparents	grandchildren
I. _ _ _ _ _ _ _ _ _ _ _ _	2. _ _ _ _ _ _ _ _ _ _ _ _

Answer the questions and make a check ☑.

9. Are you a **grandmother**?
10. ☐ Yes, I _ _.
    ☐ No, _ ' _ _ _ _.
11. ☐ I _ _ a grandmother.
    ☐ I ' _ not a grandmother.

12. Are you a **grandfather**?
13. ☐ Yes, I _ _.
    ☐ No, _ ' _ _ _ _.
14. ☐ I _ _ a grandfather.
    ☐ I'm n _ _ a grandfather.

15. Do you have any **grandchildren**?
16. ☐ Yes, I _ _.
    ☐ No, I _ _ _ ' _.

17. How many **grandsons** do you have?
18. ☐ I h _ _ _ _ grandson.
    ☐ I h _ _ _ _ grandsons.
        #
    ☐ I don't h _ _ _ any grandsons.

19. How many **granddaughters** do you have?
20. ☐ I h _ _ _ _ granddaughter.
    ☐ I h _ _ _ _ granddaughters.
        #
    ☐ I don't h _ _ _ any granddaughters.

grandmother
3. _ _ _ _ _ _ _ _ _ _ _

grandfather
4. _ _ _ _ _ _ _ _ _ _ _

mother
5. _ _ _ _ _ _ _

father
6. _ _ _ _ _ _ _

grandson
7. _ _ _ _ _ _ _ _ _ _

granddaughter
8. _ _ _ _ _ _ _ _ _ _ _ _

109

29. Copy the words.

family
— — — — — —

1. a man
— — — —

2. men
— — —

3. a woman
— — — — — — —

4. women
— — — — —

5. a child
— — — — — —

6. children
— — — — — — — —

7. a father
— — — — — — —

8. fathers
— — — — — — —

9. a mother
— — — — — — —

10. mothers
— — — — — — —

11. a grandfather
— — — — — — — — — — — —

12. grandfathers
— — — — — — — — — — —

13. a grandmother
— — — — — — — — — — — —

14. grandmothers
— — — — — — — — — — — —

15. a boy
— — — — —

16. boys
— — — —

17. a girl
— — — — — —

18. girls
— — — — —

19. a baby
— — — — — —

20. babies
— — — — — —

21. one son
— — — — — —

22. sons
— — — —

23. one daughter
— — — — — — — — —

24. daughters
— — — — — — — —

25. one brother
— — — — — — — — —

26. brothers
— — — — — — — —

27. one sister
— — — — — — — —

28. sisters
— — — — — —

29. one parent
— — — — — — — —

30. parents
— — — — — — —

31. one grandchild
— — — — — — — — — — — —

32. grandchildren
— — — — — — — — — — — — —

33. one granddaughter
— — — — — — — — — — — — — — —

34. granddaughters
— — — — — — — — — — — — — —

35. one grandson
— — — — — — — — — — — —

36. grandsons
— — — — — — — — —

37. husband
— — — — — — —

38. wife
— — — —

Family

30. Fill out the form. Please print.

☐ Mr. ☐ male ☐ female
☐ Mrs.
☐ Miss _____
       first   last
Address _____
     number   street   apt. #
_____
    city   state   zip code
☐ married ☐ single ☐ widowed ☐ divorced

31. Read these numbers.

1 one 2 two 3 three 4 four 5 five 6 six 7 seven 8 eight 9 nine 10 ten

32. Write the words.

1. one son
2. three ch_____
3. two m_n
4. one wom_n
5. four dau__t____
6. six gran_ch____r__
7. one b_b_
8. seven wom_n
9. one ch____
10. my mo_____
11. my fa_____
12. my p_r_____
13. eight g_r__
14. one m_n
15. two grand___th___
16. both g_____p_____s

17. five gr____s____
18. my w_f_
19. my h__b____
20. one br_____
21. two s_s_____
22. one gran_c_____
23. my s___s
24. my d__g_____
25. two b_b__s
26. one gra__s__
27. three gran__au_____
28. my si_____
29. my br_____s
30. six b_y_
31. my g_____m_____
32. my g_____f_____

STOP **33. Write the sentences your teacher says.**

1. _____
2. _____
3. _____
4. _____
5. _____
6. _____
7. _____

111

34. Read and copy the words.

She is	He is	They are
— — — — —	— — — —	— — — — — — —
My mother	My father	My parents
My wife	My husband	His parents
My daughter	My son	Her parents
His mother	His father	My sons
His wife	His brother	My daughters
His daughter	His son	His friends
His friend	His friend	Her friends
Her grandmother	Her grandfather	My grandparents
Her sister	Her brother	His twins
Her granddaughter	Her grandson	Her grandchildren
Her child	Her child	His children
Sally	Dan	Sally and Frank
Sue	Frank	My mother and father
Mary	John	His son and daughter
_____	_____	_____
_____	_____	_____

1. My mother is happy.
2. My father is happy.
3. My parents are happy.
4. His wife is happy.
5. Her daughter is happy.
6. Her daughters are happy.
7. Her son is happy.
8. Her sons are happy.
9. His grandmother is happy.
10. His grandmother and grandfather are happy.
11. My child is happy.
12. Her children are happy.
13. The twins are happy.
14. Her boyfriend is happy.
15. His girlfriend is happy.
16. His friend is happy.

35. Write **He**, **She**, or **They**.

1. __She__ is happy.
2. _____ is happy.
3. _____ are happy.
4. _____ is happy.
5. _____ is happy.
6. _____ are happy.
7. _____ is happy.
8. _____ are happy.
9. _____ is happy.
10. _____ are happy.
11. _____ is happy.
12. _____ are happy.
13. _____ are happy.
14. _____ is happy.
15. _____ is happy.
16. _____ is happy.

Family

36. Write **is** or **are**.

1. My mother   __is__ happy.
2. My father   _____ happy.
3. My parents   _____ happy.
4. His wife   _____ happy.
5. Her daughter   _____ happy.
6. Her daughters   _____ happy.
7. Her son   _____ happy.
8. Her sons   _____ happy.
9. His grandmother   _____ happy.
10. His grandmother and grandfather   _____ happy.
11. My child   _____ happy.
12. Her children   _____ happy.
13. The twins   _____ happy.
14. Her boyfriend   _____ happy.
15. His girlfriend   _____ happy.
16. His friend   _____ happy.

37. Write **He**, **She**, or **They** and **is** or **are**.

1. (My mother)   1. __She__ __is__ here.
2. (My brother)   2. _____ _____ fine.
3. (My brothers)   3. _____ _____ in Mexico.
4. (His wife)   4. _____ _____ angry.
5. (His grandchildren)   5. _____ _____ hungry.
6. (Her son)   6. _____ _____ thirsty.
7. (Sally)   7. _____ _____ tired.
8. (Her child)   8. _____ _____ sick.
9. (My children)   9. _____ _____ in school.
10. (My daughters)   10. _____ _____ married.
11. (His grandmother)   11. _____ _____ 93 years old.
12. (John)   12. _____ _____ my friend.
13. (John and Sue)   13. _____ _____ my friends.
14. (My teacher)   14. _____ _____ very nice.

38. Read.

39. Write <u>isn't</u> or <u>aren't</u>.

1. My wife _____ 30 years old.
2. She _____ sad.
3. Her grandchildren _____ in California.
4. They _____ brothers.
5. His daughter _____ single.
6. His daughters _____ single.
7. My son _____ married.
8. He _____ a good boy.
9. You _____ my friend.
10. We _____ friends.
11. Dan _____ here.
12. Mary _____ very happy.
13. The man _____ angry with his wife.
14. The men _____ hungry.
15. The woman _____ scared.
16. Mary and Sally _____ tired.

40. Write <u>Is</u> or <u>Are</u>.

1. _____ she scared?
2. _____ you scared?
3. _____ your son sick?
4. _____ your sons sick?
5. _____ they in the United States?
6. _____ he married?
7. _____ you going to school?
8. _____ we late?

Family

41. Read and copy the words.

She has	He has	They have
___ ___	__ ___	____ ____
My mother	My father	My parents
My wife	My husband	His parents
My daughter	My son	Her parents
His mother	His father	My sons
His wife	His brother	My daughters
His daughter	His son	His friends
His friend	His friend	Her friends
Her grandmother	Her grandfather	My grandparents
Her sister	Her brother	The twins
Her granddaughter	Her grandson	Her grandchildren
Her child	Her child	His children
Sally	Dan	Sally and Frank
Sue	Frank	My mother and father
Mary	John	His son and daughter
_____	_____	_____
_____	_____	_____

42. Write **has** or **have**.

1. She _____ $10.
2. He _____ $10.
3. They _____ $10.
4. My wife _____ $10.
5. Her daughter _____ $10.
6. Her daughters _____ $10.
7. Her son _____ $10.
8. Her sons _____ $10.
9. His grandmother _____ $10.
10. His grandmother and grandfather _____ $10.
11. My child _____ $10.
12. My children _____ $10.
13. The twins _____ $10.
14. Her boyfriend _____ $10.
15. His girlfriend _____ $10.
16. Frank _____ $10.

43. Read and copy.

I have _ _____	We have __ _____
You have ___ _____	You have ___ _____
He has __ ___	They have ____ _____
She has ___ ___	

44. Copy the words.

1. I have $5.
   _ _ _____ __.

2. She has $20.
   ____ ___ ____ __.

3. He has $10.
   __ ___ ___.

4. I have $10.
   _ _____ ___.

5. I have a big family.
   _ _____ _ ___ _____.

6. I have two sons and two daughters.
   _ _ _ _ _ _ _ _ _ _ _ _ _.

7. She has a big family.

＿ ＿＿ ＿＿＿ ＿ ＿＿＿ ＿＿＿＿＿.

8. She has two sons and two daughters.

＿＿＿ ＿＿ ＿＿＿ ＿＿＿ ＿ ＿＿＿ ＿＿＿＿＿.

9. We have two children.

＿＿ ＿＿＿ ＿＿＿ ＿＿ ＿＿＿＿＿.

10. We have one child.

＿＿ ＿＿＿＿ ＿＿＿ ＿＿＿.

11. They have two children.

＿＿＿＿ ＿＿＿ ＿＿＿ ＿＿＿＿＿＿.

12. They have one child.

＿＿＿＿ ＿＿＿ ＿＿＿ ＿＿＿.

45. Read.

I have	We have
You have	You have
He has	They have
She has	

Write **has** or **have**.

1. My daughter _____ a good husband.
2. My parents _____ an apartment.
3. I _____ one brother.
4. My son _____ $25.
5. He _____ a hamburger.
6. They _____ one son.
7. Bob _____ a red jacket.
8. We _____ three grandchildren.
9. I _____ a black pen.
10. Mrs. Lee _____ one daughter.
11. Mr. Hall _____ a new car.
12. My father _____ two sisters.
13. His parents _____ a house.
14. We _____ four grandsons.
15. She _____ a pen and a pencil.
16. Do you _____ a pen?
17. Yes. I _____ two pens.
18. Do they _____ any children?
19. No. They don't _____ any children.
20. Mary _____ a baby brother.
21. I _____ a boyfriend.
22. John and Mary _____ two children.
23. We _____ a big dog.
24. I don't _____ an umbrella.

46. Read.

1.

A: My husband has a new car.

B: A new car?

A: Yes. He has a new red car.

B: I have a red car, too.

A: Oh!

2.

A: My sister has a new baby.

B: A boy or a girl?

A: She has a baby girl.

B: How nice!

have a headache.   heart   nose

My head is very hot.   He has curly hair.
m 5'2".   I have a fever.

I'm going to the dentist.   weight

e is very tall.   I have green eyes.

CHAPTER 6

▲▲▲▲▲▲▲▲

oothache   feet

Health
and the   He is very sick.
eyes   Body

arm   earache

e has long hair.

chin   hair

hand

Do you have a stomachache?
have a backache.

weigh 110 lbs.   Her left ear hurts.

I'm going to   She is in good health.
see the doctor.   legs

Call 911! I need an ambulance.

1. Read and copy the words.

A: How are you?
B: Not so good.
A: What's wrong?
B: I have a headache.
A: Sorry to hear that.
B: Oh, that's OK.

1. I have a headache.

_ _ _ _ _ _ _ _ _ _ _ _

2. I have a stomachache.

_ _ _ _ _ _ _ _ _ _ _ _ _ _

3. I have an earache.

_ _ _ _ _ _ _ _ _ _ _ _ _

4. I have a backache.

_ _ _ _ _ _ _ _ _ _ _ _

5. I have a toothache.

_ _ _ _ _ _ _ _ _ _ _ _ _

2. Read and copy.

A: How are you?

B: Not so good.

A: What's wrong?

B: I'm sick.

_ _ _ _ _ _ _ .

A: Where are you going?

_ _ _ _ _ _ _ _ _ _ _ _ _ _ _ _ _ ?

B: I am going to the doctor.

_ _ _ _ _ _ _ _ _ _ _ _ _ _ _ _ _ .

doctor

_ _ _ _ _ _ _

3. Read and copy.

A: How are you?

B: Not so good.

A: What's wrong?

B: I have a toothache.

_ _ _ _ _ _ _ _ _ _ _ _ _ _ _ _ .

A: Where are you going?

_ _ _ _ _ _ _ _ _ _ _ _ _ _ _ _ ?

B: I'm going to the dentist.

_ _ _ _ _ _ _ _ _ _ _ _ _ _ _ _ _ _ .

dentist

_ _ _ _ _ _ _

4. Look at the pictures, and write the words.

1. How _ _ _ you?

2. Not _ _ g _ _ _ _.

3. I _ _ sick.

4. What's _ _ _ _ _?

5. I have a h _ _ _ _ _ _ _.

6. I have a s _ _ _ _ _ _ _ _ _ _.

7. I have a b _ _ _ _ _ _.

8. I have _ _ e _ _ _ _ _ _.

9. Where are you go _ _ _?

10. I am g _ _ _ _ to _ _ _ d _ _ _ _ _.

11. I have a _ _ _ _ _ _ _ _ _.

12. Where are you going?

13. I _ _ going _ _ the d _ _ _ _ _ _.

5. Copy the words.

I have

_ _ _ _ _

a cold
1. _ _ _ _ _

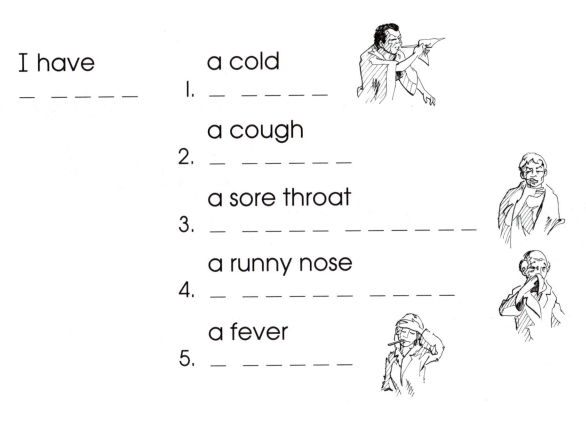

a cough
2. _ _ _ _ _ _

a sore throat
3. _ _ _ _ _ _ _ _ _ _ _

a runny nose
4. _ _ _ _ _ _ _ _ _ _

a fever
5. _ _ _ _ _ _

I am

_ _ _

sick
6. _ _ _ _

cold
7. _ _ _ _

hungry
8. _ _ _ _ _ _

tired
9. _ _ _ _ _

going to the doctor
10. _ _ _ _ _ _ _ _ _ _ _ _ _ _ _

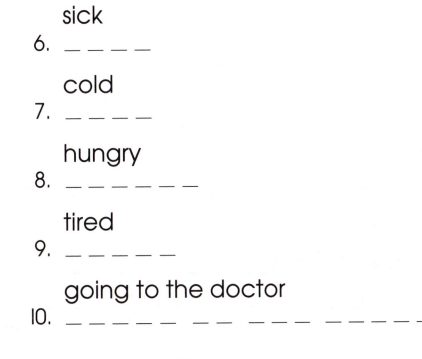

Write **am** or **have**.

11. I _ _ _ _ a cold.

12. I _ _ _ _ a runny _ _ _ _ _ .

13. I _ _ _ _ a cough.

14. I _ _ tired.

15. I _ _ _ _ a sore _ _ _ _ _ _ _ .

16. My head is very hot.

17. I _ _ _ _ a f_ _ _ _ _ .

18. I _ _ cold.

19. I _ _ very sick.

20. I _ _ not hungry.

21. I _ _ going _ _ the d_ _ _ _ _ _ .

6. Fill out the form. Please print.

☐ Mr.

☐ Mrs.

☐ Miss _____

               first   last

____male   ____female

Birthdate: _____

Date: _____

7. Read and copy the words.

the body

_ _ _   _ _ _ _

1. hair

_ _ _ _

3. ear

_ _ _

5. chin

_ _ _ _

7. neck

_ _ _ _ _

9. shoulder

_ _ _ _ _ _ _ _

11. arm

_ _ _ _

13. back

_ _ _ _ _

15. elbow

_ _ _ _ _

17. side

_ _ _ _

19. leg

_ _ _

21. ankle

_ _ _ _ _

23. heel

_ _ _ _

25. foot

_ _ _ _

27. toe

_ _ _

2. head

_ _ _ _

4. eye

_ _ _

6. nose

_ _ _ _

8. mouth

_ _ _ _ _

10. throat

_ _ _ _ _ _

12. chest

_ _ _ _ _

14. heart

_ _ _ _ _

16. stomach

_ _ _ _ _ _ _

18. wrist

_ _ _ _ _

20. thumb

_ _ _ _ _

22. hand

_ _ _ _

24. finger

_ _ _ _ _ _

26. knee

_ _ _ _

28. one lip

_ _ _   _ _ _ _

30. mouth

_ _ _   _ _ _

31. one tooth

_ _ _   _ _ _ _

29. two lips

_ _ _   _ _ _ _

32. two teeth

_ _ _   _ _ _ _

33. tongue

_ _ _ _ _ _

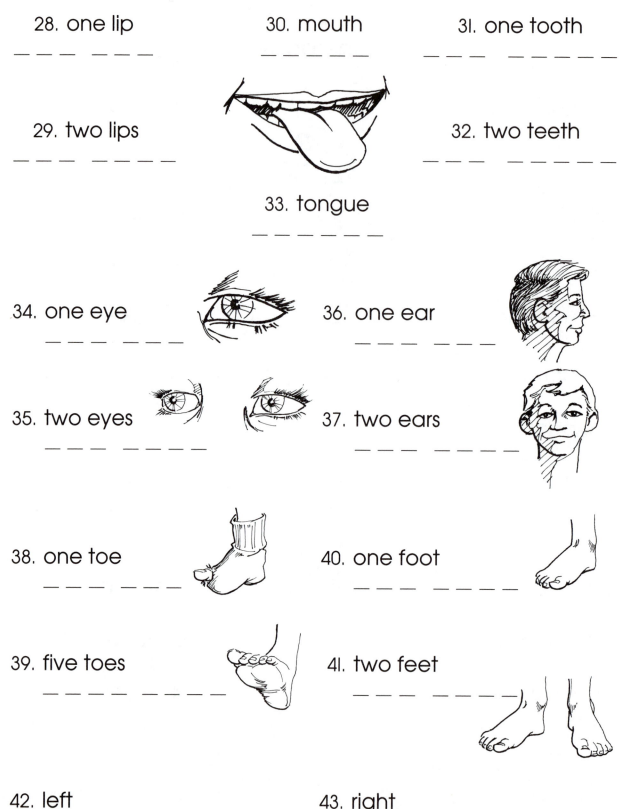

34. one eye

_ _ _   _ _ _

36. one ear

_ _ _   _ _ _

35. two eyes

_ _ _   _ _ _ _

37. two ears

_ _ _   _ _ _ _

38. one toe

_ _ _   _ _ _

40. one foot

_ _ _   _ _ _ _

39. five toes

_ _ _ _   _ _ _ _

41. two feet

_ _ _   _ _ _ _

42. left

_ _ _ _

43. right

_ _ _ _ _

8. Answer the question.

A: What hurts?

_ _ _ _ _ _ _ _ _ _ ?

B: It hurts.

_ _ _ _ _ _ _ _ .

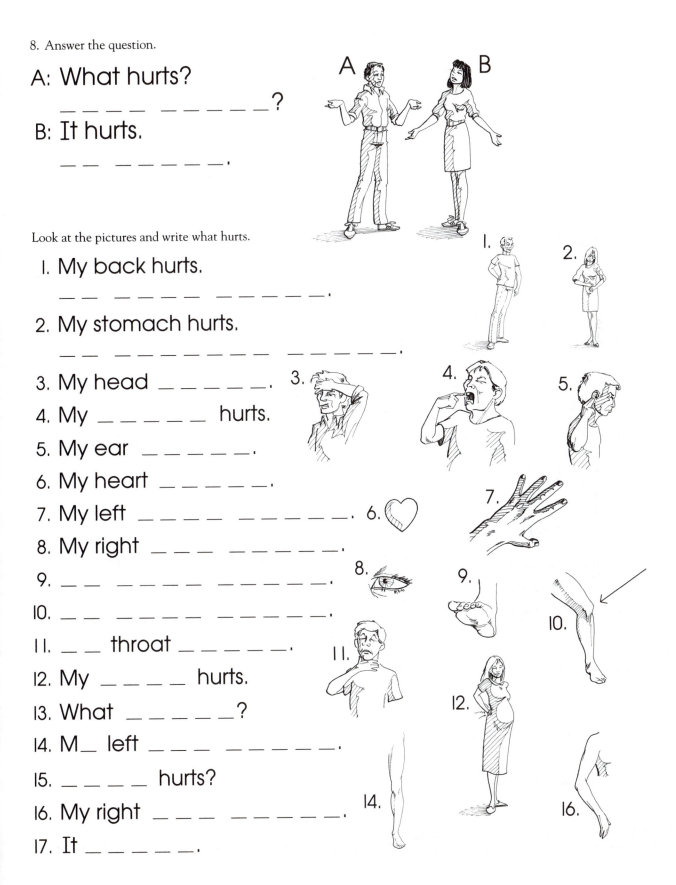

Look at the pictures and write what hurts.

1. My back hurts.

_ _ _ _ _ _ _ _ _ _ _ _ .

2. My stomach hurts.

_ _ _ _ _ _ _ _ _ _ _ _ _ _ _ .

3. My head _ _ _ _ _ _ .

4. My _ _ _ _ _ _ hurts.

5. My ear _ _ _ _ _ _ .

6. My heart _ _ _ _ _ _ .

7. My left _ _ _ _ _ _ _ _ _ _ _ .

8. My right _ _ _ _ _ _ _ _ _ .

9. _ _ _ _ _ _ _ _ _ _ _ _ _ .

10. _ _ _ _ _ _ _ _ _ _ _ _ .

11. _ _ throat _ _ _ _ _ _ .

12. My _ _ _ _ hurts.

13. What _ _ _ _ _ _ ?

14. M_ left _ _ _ _ _ _ _ _ _ .

15. _ _ _ _ _ hurts?

16. My right _ _ _ _ _ _ _ _ _ .

17. It _ _ _ _ _ _ .

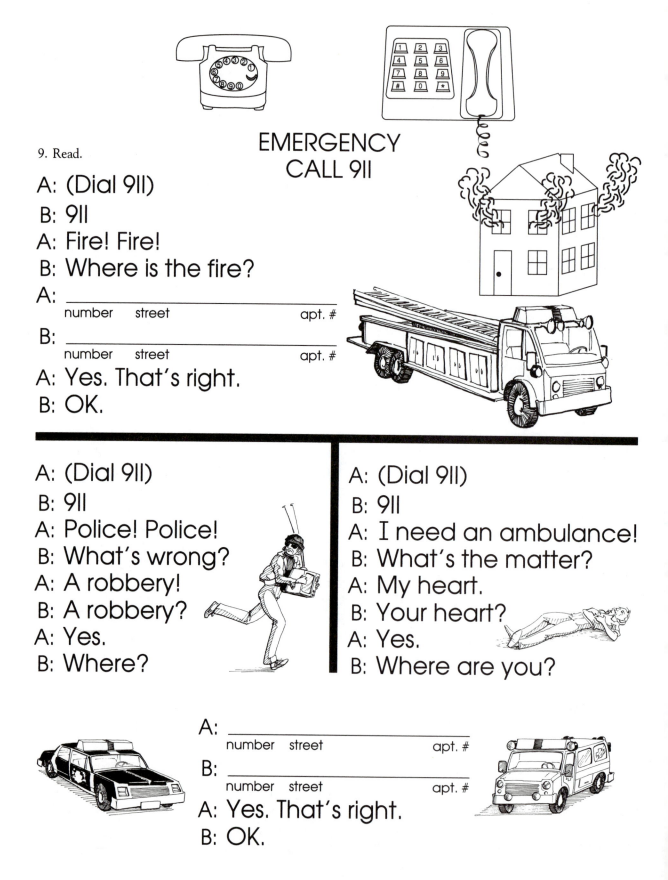

EMERGENCY CALL 911

9. Read.

A: (Dial 911)
B: 911
A: Fire! Fire!
B: Where is the fire?
A: _____
    number   street   apt. #
B: _____
    number   street   apt. #
A: Yes. That's right.
B: OK.

A: (Dial 911)
B: 911
A: Police! Police!
B: What's wrong?
A: A robbery!
B: A robbery?
A: Yes.
B: Where?

A: (Dial 911)
B: 911
A: I need an ambulance!
B: What's the matter?
A: My heart.
B: Your heart?
A: Yes.
B: Where are you?

A: _____
    number   street   apt. #
B: _____
    number   street   apt. #
A: Yes. That's right.
B: OK.

10. Copy the words.

1. Her ___

2. His ___

What hurts?

_ _ _ _   _ _ _ _ _?

My foot hurts.
His foot hurts.
Her foot hurts.

1. Her head hurts.

_ _ _   _ _ _ _ _   _ _ _ _ _.

2. His right foot hurts.

_ _ _   _ _ _ _ _   _ _ _ _   _ _ _ _ _.

3. Her   left   ear   hurts.

_ _ _   _ _ _ _   _ _ _   _ _ _ _ _.

4. His   left   hurts.

_ _ _   _ _ _ _   _ _ _   _ _ _ _ _.

Look at the pictures and write the words.

5. H_ _   _ _ _ _   hurts.

6. H_ _   r_ _ _ _ _   _ _ _   _ _ _ _ _.

7. _ _ _   _ _ _ _ _ _   _ _ _   _ _ _ _ _.

8. _ _ _   l_ _ _   _ _ _ _   _ _ _ _ _.

9. _ _ _   left   _ _ _ _ _ _ _   _ _ _ _ _.

10. _ _ _   st_ _ _ _ _   _ _ _ _ _.

11. What   _ _ _ _ _ _?

12. _ _ _   k_ _ _   _ _ _ _ _.

13. _ _ _ _   hurts?

14. _ _ _   l_ _ _   _ _ _   _ _ _ _ _.

131

11. Copy the words.

What hurts?

1. _ _ _ _   _ _ _ _ _?

My feet hurt.
My hands hurt.
They hurt.

My   His   Her

2. _ _   3. _ _ _   4. _ _ _

feet
5. _ _ _ _

teeth
6. _ _ _ _ _

eyes
7. _ _ _ _

arms
8. _ _ _ _

wrists
9. _ _ _ _ _ _

hands
10. _ _ _ _ _

fingers
11. _ _ _ _ _ _ _

knees
12. _ _ _ _ _

elbows
13. _ _ _ _ _ _

ankles
14. _ _ _ _ _ _

toes
15. _ _ _ _

legs
16. _ _ _ _

heels
17. _ _ _ _ _

shoulders
18. _ _ _ _ _ _ _ _ _

thumbs
19. _ _ _ _ _ _

hurt
20. _ _ _ _

132

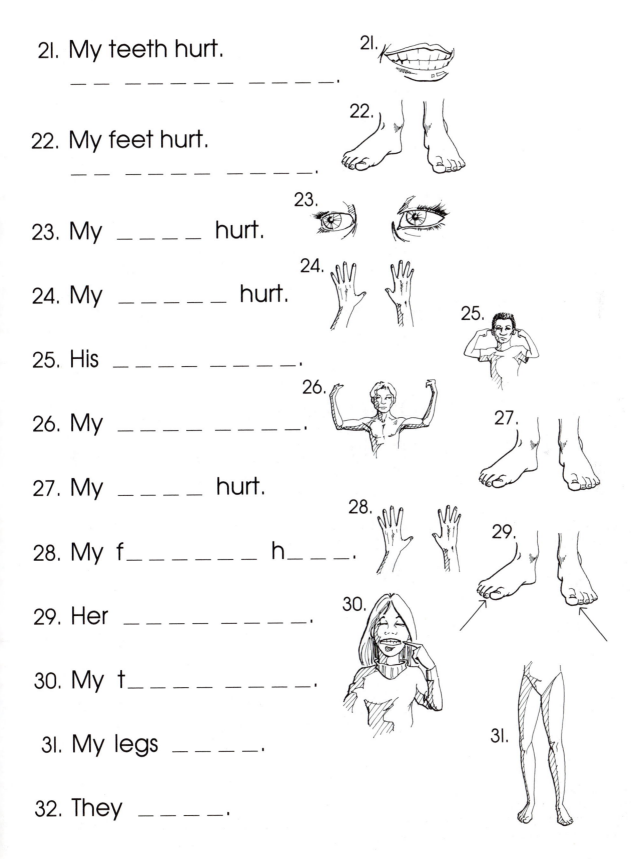

21. My teeth hurt.

_ _ _ _ _ _ _ _ _ _ _ _ .

22. My feet hurt.

_ _ _ _ _ _ _ _ _ _ .

23. My _ _ _ _ hurt.

24. My _ _ _ _ _ _ hurt.

25. His _ _ _ _ _ _ _ _ _ .

26. My _ _ _ _ _ _ _ _ _ .

27. My _ _ _ _ hurt.

28. My f _ _ _ _ _ _ _ h _ _ _ .

29. Her _ _ _ _ _ _ _ _ _ .

30. My t _ _ _ _ _ _ _ _ _ .

31. My legs _ _ _ _ _ .

32. They _ _ _ _ _ .

12. Read.

| What hurts? | It hurts. | They hurt. |

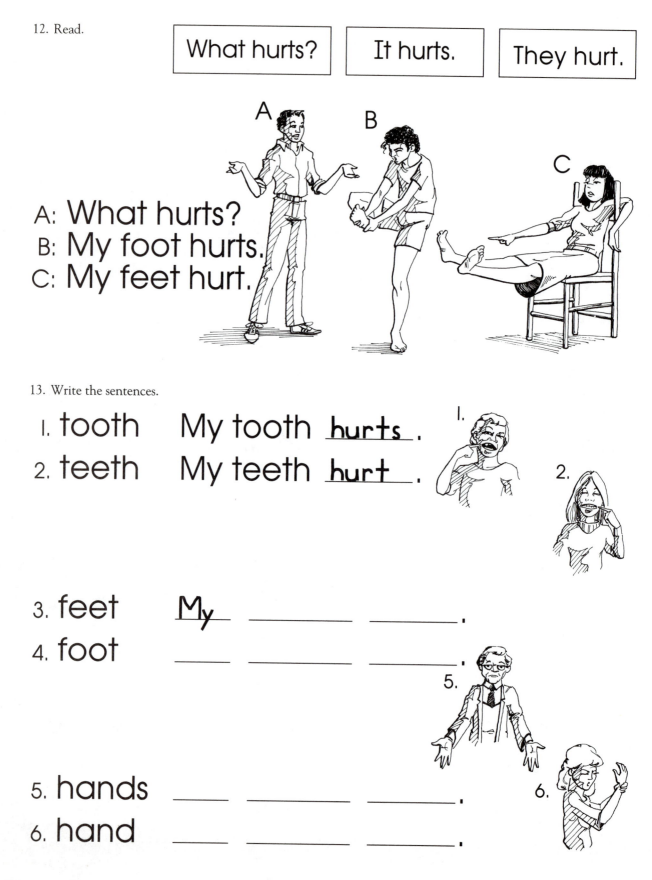

A: What hurts?
B: My foot hurts.
C: My feet hurt.

13. Write the sentences.

1. tooth   My tooth __hurts__ .

2. teeth   My teeth __hurt__ .

3. feet   __My__ _____ _____ .

4. foot   ___ _____ _____ .

5. hands   ___ _____ _____ .

6. hand   ___ _____ _____ .

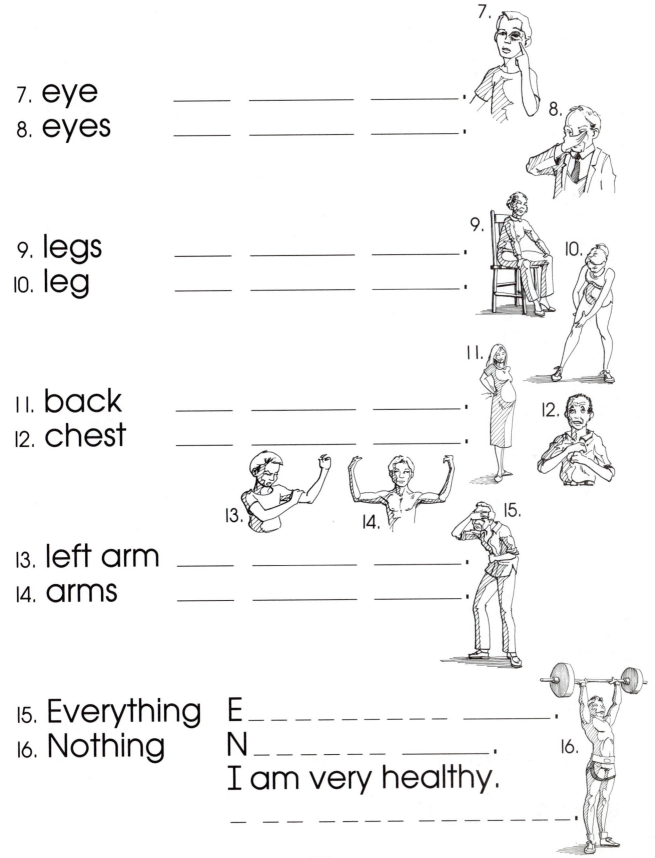

7. eye _____ _____ _____ .
8. eyes _____ _____ _____ .

9. legs _____ _____ _____ .
10. leg _____ _____ _____ .

11. back _____ _____ _____ .
12. chest _____ _____ _____ .

13. left arm _____ _____ _____ .
14. arms _____ _____ _____ .

15. Everything E_ _ _ _ _ _ _ _ _ _ _ _ _ _ _ _ .
16. Nothing N_ _ _ _ _ _ _ _ _ _ _ .
I am very healthy.

_ _ _ _ _ _ _ _ _ _ _ _ .

14. Read these words.

h	wh	s	g	th
How hurt hurts hear head	What What's Where	so sick sorry	good going	the That's that

A

B

Fill in the words.

A: How _ _ _ you?

B: _ _ _ so good.

A: What's w _ _ _ _?

B: I _ _ sick.

A: Where _ _ _ you going?

B: I'm _ _ _ _ _ to the d _ _ _ _ _ _.

A: W _ _ _ hurts?

B: My head _ _ _ _ _ _ and my eyes _ _ _ _ _.

A: I'm sorry to _ _ _ _ that.

B: Oh, t _ _ _ '_ OK.

15. Read.

A: What color is your hair?
B: I have black hair.
C: I have gray hair.
D: I have blond hair.
E: I have white hair.
F: I have brown hair.

B C D E F

A

16. Make a check ☑ and copy the words.

1. What **color** is your hair?

2. ☐ brown   ☐ blond   ☐ red

   _ _ _ _ _   _ _ _ _ _   _ _ _

   ☐ black   ☐ gray   ☐ white

   _ _ _ _ _   _ _ _ _   _ _ _ _ _

3. I have _____ hair.

4. ☐ a little   ☐ no hair

   _ _ _ _ _ _ _ _   _ _ _ _ _ _

   ☐ long   ☐ short

   _ _ _ _   _ _ _ _ _

5. I have _____ hair.

6. ☐ straight   ☐ wavy

   _ _ _ _ _ _ _ _   _ _ _ _

   ☐ curly

   _ _ _ _ _

7. I have _____ hair.

17. Write the words and make a check ✔.

1. What color _ _ your hair?

2. I _ _ _ _ _____ hair.

3. Do you have **long** hair?   ☐ Yes, I do.
                                    ☐ No, I don't.

4. Do you have **short** hair?   ☐ Yes, I do.
                                    ☐ No, I don't.

5. Do you have **straight** hair? ☐ Yes, I do.
                                    ☐ No, I don't.

6. Do you have **wavy** hair?   ☐ Yes, I do.
                                    ☐ No, I don't.

7. Do you have **curly** hair?   ☐ Yes, I do.
                                    ☐ No, I don't.

8. HAIR _____
        (color)

18. Read and copy.

| I have |
| 1. _ _ _ _ _ |
| You have |
| 2. _ _ _ _ _ _ _ |

| He has |
| 3. _ _ _ _ _ |
| She has |
| 4. _ _ _ _ _ _ |

A B C

A: What color are your eyes?
B: I have brown eyes.
C: She has brown eyes.

19. Make a check ☑ and write the words.

1. What color are your eyes?
2. ☐ I have **brown** eyes.   ☐ I have **blue** eyes.
   ☐ I have **black** eyes.   ☐ I have **green** eyes.
3. What c_ _ _ _ are your eyes?
4. I h_ _ _ _____ eyes.
   (color)
5. Do you have **brown** eyes? ☐ Yes, I _ _.
                                ☐ No, I _ _ _'_.
6. Do you have **black** eyes? ☐ Yes, I _ _.
                                ☐ No, I _ _ _'_.
7. Do you have **blue** eyes?   ☐ Yes, I _ _.
                                ☐ No, I _ _ _'_.
8. Do you have **green** eyes? ☐ Yes, I _ _.
                                ☐ No, I _ _ _'_.

20. Write <u>have</u> or <u>has</u>.

1. I _____ brown eyes.
2. She _____ blue eyes.
3. He _____ green eyes.
4. My husband _____ brown eyes.
5. I _ _ _ _ _____ eyes and _____ hair.
6. HAIR _____
        (color)
7. EYES _____
        (color)

21. Read.

HEIGHT

_ _ _ _ _ _

A: How tall are you?
B: I'm 5'2".
A: You are very short.
B: Yes, I am.

22. Write the words and make a check ☑.

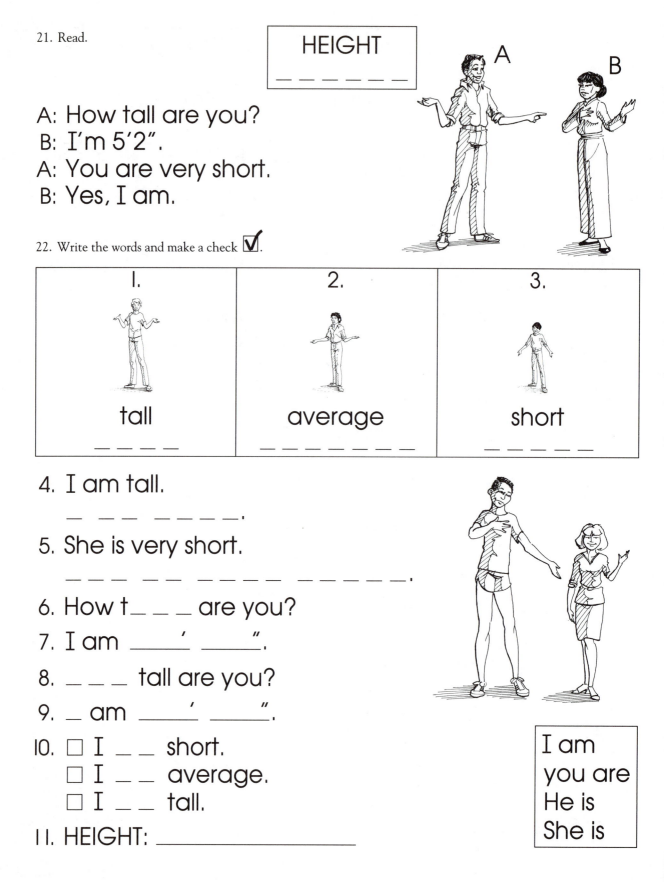

1.	2.	3.
tall	average	short
_ _ _ _	_ _ _ _ _ _ _	_ _ _ _ _ _

4. I am tall.

 _ _ __ _ _ _ _.

5. She is very short.

 _ _ __ __ _ _ _ _ _ _ _ _.

6. How t_ _ _ are you?

7. I am ____' ____".

8. _ _ _ tall are you?

9. _ am ____' ____".

10. ☐ I _ _ short.
    ☐ I _ _ average.
    ☐ I _ _ tall.

11. HEIGHT: _____

I am
you are
He is
She is

140

23. Read.

A: How tall are you?
B: I'm 5'7".
C: I'm 5'7".
A: You are the same height.
B: Yes.
C: We are the same height.

A

B   C

HEIGHT: 5'7"   HEIGHT: 5'7"

Answer the questions.

1. How tall is he?
2. He _ _ ____' ____".
3. How tall is she?
4. She _ _ ____' ____".
5. How tall are they?
6. They _ _ _ the _ _ _ _ _ _ _ _ _ _ _.

| We **are** |
| You **are** |
| They **are** |

24. Fill in this I.D. card.

NAME _____
          first   middle   last
ADDRESS _____
          no.   street   apt. #

          _____
          city   state   zip code
SEX   HAIR   EYES   HEIGHT

____   ____   ____   ____

25. Read.

STOP

26. Write.

1. 5'1"
2. 6'2"
3. I am 5'.
4. 4'8"
5. He is 5'5".

1. _____
2. _____
3. _____
4. _____
5. _____
6. _____

27. Read.

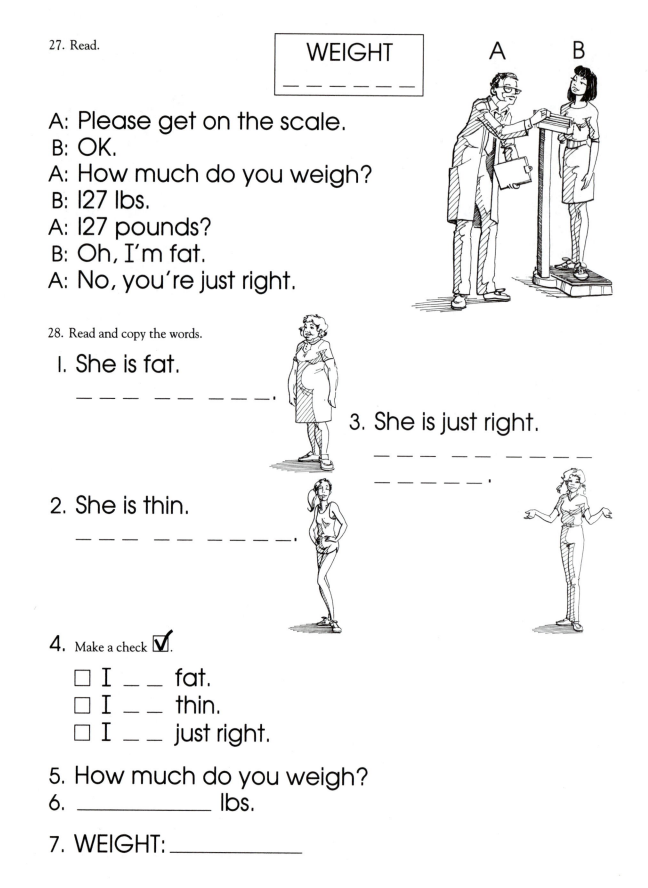

WEIGHT

_ _ _ _ _ _ _

A   B

A: Please get on the scale.
B: OK.
A: How much do you weigh?
B: 127 lbs.
A: 127 pounds?
B: Oh, I'm fat.
A: No, you're just right.

28. Read and copy the words.

1. She is fat.

_ _ _ _ _ _ _ _ _ _.

2. She is thin.

_ _ _ _ _ _ _ _ _ _.

3. She is just right.

_ _ _ _ _ _ _ _ _ _
_ _ _ _ _ _ _ .

4. Make a check ☑.

☐ I _ _ fat.
☐ I _ _ thin.
☐ I _ _ just right.

5. How much do you weigh?
6. _____ lbs.

7. WEIGHT: _____

29. Read.

A: How much do you weigh?
B: 110 lbs.
C: 110 lbs.
A: You are the same weight.
B: Yes.
C: We are the same weight.

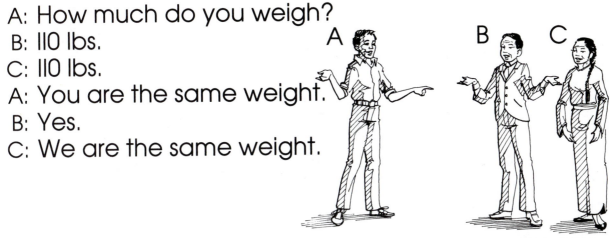

A   B   C

WEIGHT: 110 lbs.   WEIGHT: 110 lbs.

30. Fill in this I.D. card.

NAME _____
         first   middle   last

ADDRESS _____
         no.   street   apt. #

         _____
         city   state   zip code

SEX   HAIR   EYES   HEIGHT   WEIGHT

_____   _____   _____   _____   _____

31. Read.

1. 130 lbs.
2. 155 lbs.
3. 115 lbs.
4. 100 lbs.
5. 183 lbs.

STOP

32. Write what your teacher says.

1. _____
2. _____
3. _____
4. _____
5. _____

33. Practice writing the letters in your name.

signature
– – – – – – – – –

𝒶A   ℬB   𝒞C   𝒟D

ℰE   ℱF   𝒢G   ℋH

𝒥I   𝒥J   𝒦K   ℒL

ℳM   𝓃N   𝒪O   𝒫P

𝒬Q   ℛR   𝒮S   𝒥T

𝒰U   𝒱V   𝒲W   𝒳X

𝒴Y   𝒵Z

a b c d e f g h i

j k l m n o p q

r s t u v w x y z

Print your name.

first   last

Sign your name.

first   last

Signature

first   last

34. Please print.

☐ Mr.

☐ Mrs.

☐ Miss

ADDRESS

LAST	FIRST	MIDDLE

NUMBER STREET	APT. #

CITY	STATE	ZIP CODE

☐ MALE   ☐ FEMALE

☐ SINGLE   ☐ MARRIED   ☐ WIDOWED   ☐ DIVORCED

HAIR _____   EYES _____   HEIGHT _____   WEIGHT _____

LANGUAGE/S _____

PLACE OF BIRTH (COUNTRY) _____

DATE OF BIRTH _____

AGE _____

TELEPHONE NUMBER _ _ _-_ _ _ _

SOCIAL SECURITY NUMBER _ _ _-_ _-_ _ _ _

DATE _____

SIGNATURE _____

35. Read and copy the words.

H h

1. head

2. hurt

3. hand

4. hurts

5. have

6. headache

7. He

8. has

9. hair

10. hungry

11. heel

12. His

13. heart

14. hot

15. husband

16. height

I'm 5'6".

We are the same **height**.

Write your

NAME	_____
WEIGHT	_____
HEIGHT	_____

17. homesick

El Salvador

Mexico

I'm **homesick**.
I think about my country,
and I'm sad.

China   Vietnam

H h

head	have	hair	hot
hurt	headache	hungry	husband
hurts	He	heel	height
hand	has	heart	homesick

36. Read.

My wife	has a cold.
Ann	has a cold.
She	has a cold.

My husband	has a good job.
Bill	has a good job.
He	has a good job.

37. Write **has** or **have**.

1. I _____ a stomachache.
2. My daughter _____ curly hair.
3. She _____ a headache.
4. My son _____ brown eyes.
5. He _____ two daughters.
6. I _____ a runny nose.
7. His girlfriend _____ a cold.
8. I _____ two children.
9. Bill _____ a toothache.
10. Her sister _____ long hair.
11. Ann _____ an earache.
12. He _____ a book.
13. I _____ a cough.
14. Mrs. Lopez _____ long black hair.
15. My wife _____ green eyes.
16. My brother _____ two children
17. Mary _____ straight blond hair.
18. I don't _____ any children.
19. He _____ four sons.
20. Dan _____ two brothers.
21. I _____ a backache.
22. Her husband _____ a new car.
23. She _____ a sore throat.
24. His son _____ a fever.
25. Miss Wong _____ a boyfriend.
26. The baby _____ a little hair.

> I **have**
> You **have**
> He **has**
> She **has**

38. Read and copy the words.

S s

My **sister** is **sick**.

1. sick

2. sister

3. sisters

My **sisters** are scared.

4. signature

Sign your name.

Name		
	FIRST	LAST
Address		
	NO. STREET	APT. #
	CITY	STATE	ZIP CODE
Date		
Signature		

5. sore

She has a **sore** throat.

Sorry I'm late.

6. sorry

Sh sh

She is short.

7. She

8. short

9. shoulder

My **shoulder** hurts.

This **shirt** is $15.

10. shirt

S	sick sister sisters signature sign sore sorry
Sh	she short shoulder shirt

39. Read and copy the words.

St st

1. stomach

2. stomachache

Her **stomach** hurts.
She has a **stomachache**.

3. stop

Stop at the sign.

4. state

I live in California.

What **state** do you live in?   B

A   C   I live in New York.

5. stamp

I need an airmail **stamp**.

Please **stand up**.

6. stand up

St	stomach	stomachache	stop
st	state	stamp	stand up

40. Read and copy the words.

Str str

1. straight

2. street

Str str   straight street

41. Read.

I **have**	We **have**
You **have**	You **have**
He **has**	They **have**
She **has**	

We	have brown eyes.
My friend and I	have brown eyes.
Maria and I	have brown eyes.

They	have a small apartment.
My mother and father	have a small apartment.
My parents	have a small apartment.

42. Write **We** or **They**.

(My mother and I)	1. __**We**__	are thin.
(My mother and father)	2. _____	have a big house.
(My parents)	3. _____	live in Mexico.
(My friends and I)	4. _____	speak Spanish.
(My sister and I)	5. _____	are twins.
(My children)	6. _____	are healthy.
(My children and I)	7. _____	have short hair.
(My children)	8. _____	have short hair.
(My son and I)	9. _____	want two Cokes.
(Mr. and Mrs. Lee)	10. _____	are late.
(My brother and I)	11. _____	have black cars.

43. Write **has** or **have**.

1. We _____ two small children.

2. They _____ two grandsons.

3. My husband and I _____ one son.

4. My husband _____ black hair.

5. My grandparents _____ one grandchild.

6. We don't _____ any money.

7. She _____ $42.

8. They don't _____ any children.

9. They _____ a little girl.

10. My brother and I _____ green eyes.

11. I don't _____ any sisters.

12. We _____ one daughter.

13. My mother and father _____ an apartment.

44. Read and copy the words.

T t

1. tooth

2. toothache

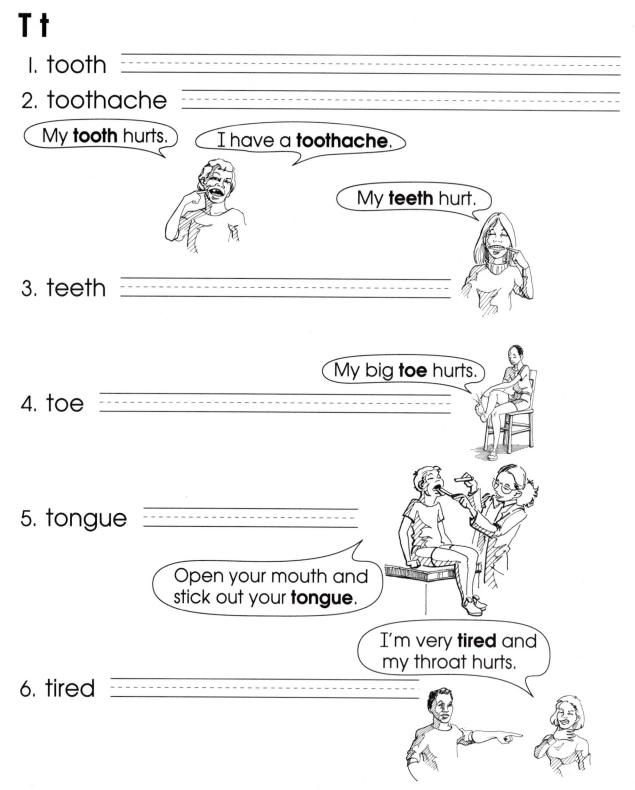

3. teeth

4. toe

5. tongue

6. tired

7. tall

My brother is very **tall**.

8. teacher

My **teacher** is very nice.

9. turn

10. television

Turn the **TV** off.

11. Tuesday

No school Monday.
See you **Tuesday**.

T t

| tooth | toothache | teeth | toe | tongue | tired |
| tall | teacher | turn | television | TV | Tuesday |

45. Read and copy the words.

Th th

1. thin

2. think

3. thumb

4. thirty

5. thirsty

6. Thursday

Bye. See you **Thursday**.

7. Thank

Here is your change.

Thank you.

thr

8. throat

I have a sore **throat**.

9. three 3

We have **three** children.

Th th						
thin	think	thumb	thirty	thirsty	Thursday	thank
Thr thr	throat	three				

46. Read.

She is

Sue
Jane
Sally
Mary
Ann
Mrs. Green
Miss Brown

_____

_____

I am a teacher.
My mother is a teacher.
Sally is a teacher.
She is a teacher.

He is

Dan
John
Frank
Bob
Bill
Mr. Green
Dr. Chan

_____

I am a doctor.
Her father is a doctor.
Frank is a doctor.
He is a doctor.

47. Write **am** or **is**.

1. I ___**am**___ sick.
2. She _____ going to the doctor.
3. He _____ tall.
4. I _____ healthy.
5. Bob _____ short.
6. My daughter _____ thin.
7. Sue _____ my friend.
8. His girlfriend _____ 25 years old.
9. I _____ very tired.
10. Her father _____ fine.
11. I _____ going to the dentist.
12. He _____ not thirsty.
13. Jane _____ married.
14. My daughter _____ 5'6".
15. He _____ 56 years old.
16. I _____ very happy to see you.
17. Mrs. Green _____ my teacher.
18. Mr. Green _____ her husband.

> I **am**
> You **are**
> He **is**
> She **is**

48. Read and copy the words.

B b

1. back

2. backache

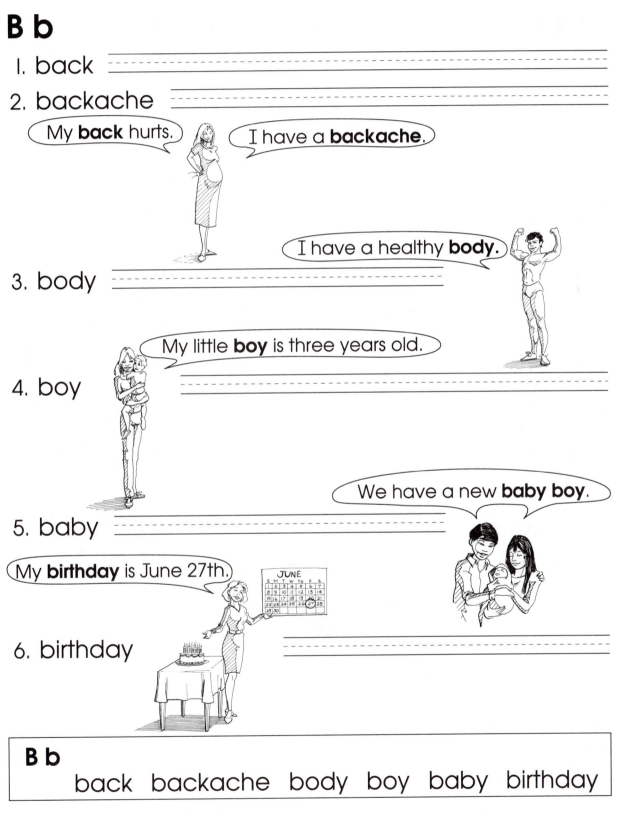

My **back** hurts.

I have a **backache**.

I have a healthy **body**.

3. body

My little **boy** is three years old.

4. boy

We have a new **baby boy**.

5. baby

My **birthday** is June 27th.

JUNE

6. birthday

B b

back   backache   body   boy   baby   birthday

---

49. Read and copy the words.

Br br

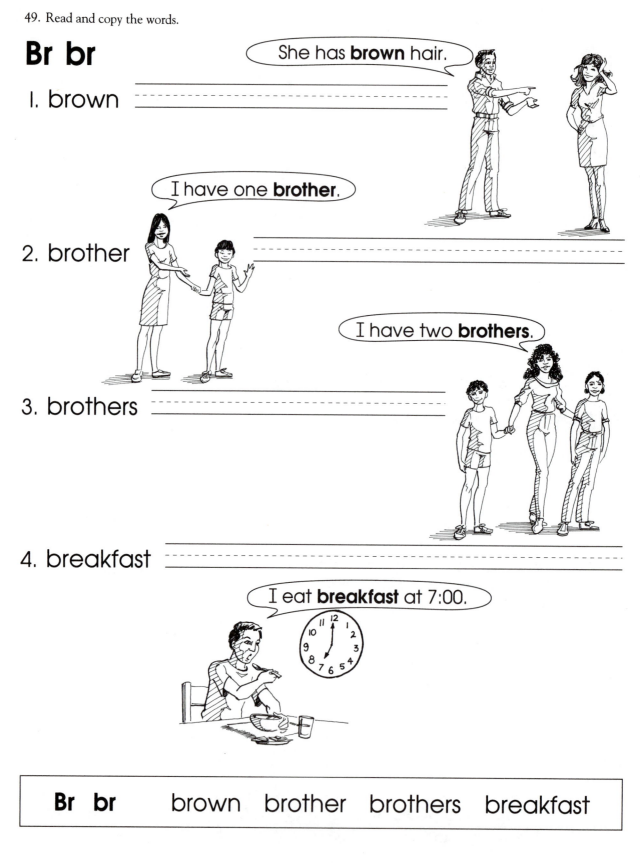

1. brown _____

2. brother _____

3. brothers _____

4. breakfast _____

Br br	brown brother brothers breakfast

50. Read and copy the words.

Bl bl

1. blue

He has **blue** eyes.

2. black

She has a **black** car.

3. blond

My sister has **blond** hair.

4. blouse

My **blouse** is **blue** and white.

| **Bl bl** | blue | black | blond | blouse |

51. Read and copy.

1.
It is
_ _ _ _

2.
It's
_ _ ' _

I am
you are
He is
She is
It is

Read.

3. What time is it?
4. It's 6:00.
5. It's 6:30.

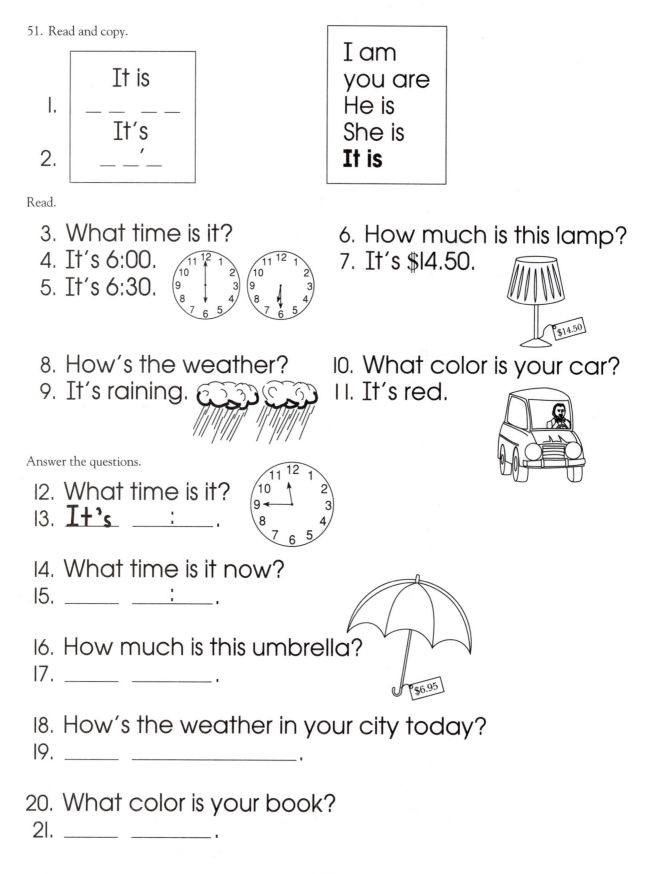

6. How much is this lamp?
7. It's $14.50.

8. How's the weather?
9. It's raining.

10. What color is your car?
11. It's red.

Answer the questions.

12. What time is it?
13. It's ___ : ___.

14. What time is it now?
15. _____ ___ : ___.

16. How much is this umbrella?
17. _____ _____.

18. How's the weather in your city today?
19. _____ _____.

20. What color is your book?
21. _____ _____.

52. Read and copy the words.

C c

1. cold

2. cough

3. curly

C c	cold	cough	curly

53. Read and copy the words.

Ch ch

1. chin

2. chest

3. child

4. children

5. chicken

Ch ch   chin   chest   child   children   chicken

54. Read.

I **am**	We **are**
You **are**	You **are**
He **is**	They **are**
She **is**	
It **is**	

Write <u>am</u>, <u>is</u>, or <u>are</u>.

1. I _____ fine, thank you.
2. She _____ my wife.
3. We _____ husband and wife.
4. They _____ happy.
5. You _____ a good teacher.
6. My brother _____ 45 years old.
7. He _____ in Los Angeles.
8. My sisters _____ in New York.
9. My friend and I _____ the same age.
10. It _____ 12 noon.
11. My sister _____ 5'2".
12. My brothers _____ in China.
13. Tom and I _____ friends.
14. I _____ very short.
15. It _____ 10:30.
16. My parents _____ tall.
17. Bob and Sue _____ the same height.
18. It _____ hot and sunny.
19. Her son _____ a healthy boy.
20. They _____ going to the doctor.
21. My apartment _____ white.
22. I _____ not homesick.
23. You _____ not late.
24. She _____ not thirsty.
25. He _____ not single.
26. It _____ not raining.
27. We _____ not going to the supermarket.
28. They _____ not in the United States.

55. Read and copy the words.

R r

1. right — This is my **right** hand.

2. runny — I have a **runny** nose.

3. raining — It's **raining**. How's the weather?

4. red — She has a **red** sweater.

5. robbery — What's the matter? It's a **robbery**.

6. radio — Please turn the **radio** on.

R r	right runny raining red robbery radio

56. Write <u>do</u>, <u>don't</u>, or <u>have</u>.

1. Do Sally and Frank have any children?
2. Yes, they _____ .
3. They _____ two sons.

4. Do your parents have an apartment?
5. No, they _____ .
6. They _____ a big house.

7. Do you have the books?
8. No, we _____ .
9. We don't _____ the books.

10. Do you have any brothers?
11. Yes, I _____ .
12. I _____ one brother.

57. Answer the question with <u>am</u>, <u>I'm</u>, <u>is</u>, <u>isn't</u>, <u>are</u>, <u>aren't</u>.

1. Are you sick?
2. No, I _____ not.
3. _____ not sick.
4. I _____ healthy.

5. Are your parents in China?
6. Yes, they _____ .
7. They _____ in China.

8. Is she tall?
9. No, she _____ .
10. She _____ short.

11. Are your parents in the U.S.?
12. No, they _____ .
13. They _____ in Mexico.

14. Is your brother tall?
15. No, he _____ .
16. He _____ average.

58. Write the words and check one ✓.

1. ☐ I _____ a man.
   ☐ I _____ a woman.
2. ☐ I _____ married. ☐ I _____ single. ☐ I _____ widowed.
3. How old are you? I _____ _____ years old.
4. ☐ My teacher _____ a man. His name is _____.
   ☐ My teacher _____ a woman. Her name is _____.
5. Please **print** your name. _____
6. Please **sign** your name. _____

59. Match the questions with the correct answers. Write the letters on the lines.

H	1. What's your name?	A. 648-7382
_____	2. What's your address?	B. 8:30
_____	3. What's your telephone number?	C. 29 years old
_____	4. What's your Social Security Number?	D. 5'7"
_____	5. How old are you?	E. 925 16th St. #3
_____	6. How much do you weigh?	F. China
_____	7. How tall are you?	G. 565-32-1074
_____	8. What country are you from?	H. John Lee
_____	9. What language do you speak?	I. 150 lbs.
_____	10. What time is it?	J. Chinese

Health and the Body

60. Match the questions with the correct answers. Write the letters on the lines.

_____ 1. How many children do you have?

_____ 2. How are you?

_____ 3. Where are you going?

_____ 4. What's wrong?

_____ 5. How much is this book?

_____ 6. When is your birthday?

_____ 7. What color is the American flag?

_____ 8. How's the weather?

_____ 9. Are you married?

_____ 10. When is your appointment?

A. Fine, thank you.

B. $9.95

C. red, white, and blue

D. one son and two daughters

E. Yes, I am.

F. Friday, October 14, at 3:45 p.m.

G. June 27th

H. It's sunny today.

I. I'm going to the dentist.

J. I have a toothache.

Alphabet and Number Reference Guide

PRINT.

A B C D E F G H I J K L M

N O P Q R S T U V W X Y Z

print.

a b c d e f g h i j k l m

n o p q r s t u v w x y z

Write.

Aa	Bb	Cc	Dd	Ee	Ff
Gg	Hh	Ii	Jj	Kk	Ll
Mm	Nn	Oo	Pp	Qq	Rr
Ss	Tt	Uu	Vv	Ww	Xx
Yy	Zz				

NUMBERS.

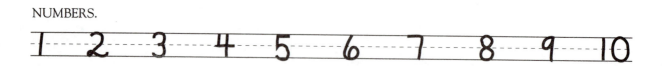

1 2 3 4 5 6 7 8 9 10